Jochen Schneider, Thomas Strothotte, Winfried Marotzki (Eds.)

**Computational Visualistics, Media Informatics,
and Virtual Communities**

W0080373

Bildwissenschaft

Herausgegeben von
Klaus Sachs-Hombach und Klaus Rehkämper

Editorial Board

Prof. Dr. Horst Bredekamp
Humboldt-Universität Berlin

PD Dr. Dagmar Schmauks
Technische Universität Berlin

Prof. Dr. Ferdinand Fellmann
Universität Chemnitz

Prof. Dr. Wolfgang Schnotz
Universität Koblenz-Landau

Prof. Dr. Christopher Habel
Universität Hamburg

Prof. Dr. Oliver Scholz
Universität Münster

Dr. John Hyman
The Queen's College Oxford

Prof. Dr. Thomas Strothotte
Universität Magdeburg

Prof. Dr. Wolfgang Kemp
Universität Hamburg

Prof. Dr. Michael Sukale
Universität Oldenburg

Prof. Dr. Karlheinz Lüdeking
Akademie der bildenden Künste Nürnberg

Prof. Dr. Bernd Weidenmann
Universität der Bundeswehr München

Prof. Dr. Roland Posner
Technische Universität Berlin

Prof. Dr. Ute Werner
Universität Karlsruhe (TH)

Prof. Dr. Claus Rollinger
Universität Osnabrück

Prof. Dr. Dieter Wiedemann
Hochschule für Film und Fernsehen Potsdam

Zunehmend werden unsere Erfahrungen und Erkenntnisse durch Bilder vermittelt und geprägt. In kaum zu überschätzender Weise halten Bilder Einzug in Alltag und Wissenschaft. Gemessen an der Bedeutung, die bildhaften Darstellungen mittlerweile zugeschrieben wird, erstaunt jedoch die bisher ausgebliebene Institutionalisierung einer allgemeinen Bildwissenschaft.

Mit dieser Buchreihe möchten die Herausgeber einen transdisziplinären Rahmen für die Bemühungen der einzelnen mit Bildern beschäftigten Fachdisziplinen zur Verfügung stellen und so einen Beitrag zum Entstehen einer allgemeinen Bildwissenschaft leisten.

Jochen Schneider, Thomas Strothotte,
Winfried Marotzki (Eds.)

Computational Visualistics, Media Informatics, and Virtual Communities

Deutscher Universitäts-Verlag

Bibliografische Information Der Deutschen Bibliothek
Die Deutsche Bibliothek verzeichnet diese Publikation in der Deutschen Nationalbibliografie;
detaillierte bibliografische Daten sind im Internet über <http://dnb.ddb.de> abrufbar.

Band 11 der Reihe Bildwissenschaft, die bis 2001 im Scriptum Verlag, Magdeburg erschienen
ist.

1. Auflage Dezember 2003

Alle Rechte vorbehalten
© Deutscher Universitäts-Verlag/GWV Fachverlage GmbH, Wiesbaden 2003

Lektorat: Ute Wrasmann / Frauke Schindler

Der Deutsche Universitäts-Verlag ist ein Unternehmen von Springer Science+Business Media.
www.duv.de

Das Werk einschließlich aller seiner Teile ist urheberrechtlich geschützt.
Jede Verwertung außerhalb der engen Grenzen des Urheberrechtsgesetzes
ist ohne Zustimmung des Verlags unzulässig und strafbar. Das gilt insbe-
sondere für Vervielfältigungen, Übersetzungen, Mikroverfilmungen und die
Einspeicherung und Verarbeitung in elektronischen Systemen.

Die Wiedergabe von Gebrauchsnamen, Handelsnamen, Warenbezeichnungen usw. in diesem
Werk berechtigt auch ohne besondere Kennzeichnung nicht zu der Annahme, dass solche
Namen im Sinne der Warenzeichen- und Markenschutz-Gesetzgebung als frei zu betrachten
wären und daher von jedermann benutzt werden dürften.

Umschlaggestaltung: Regine Zimmer, Dipl.-Designerin, Frankfurt/Main

Gedruckt auf säurefreiem und chlorfrei gebleichtem Papier

ISBN-13:978-3-8244-4550-9   e-ISBN-13:978-3-322-81318-3
DOI: 10.1007/978-3-322-81318-3

Preface

In recent years there has been a rising awareness within the international scientific community that there is a need to study the various aspects of the integration of images and new media both from the point of view of computer science as well as from other areas which deal with users' interface to information sources, in particular design, psychology, education, political science, sociology, and philosophy.

To a certain extent the view of the topic from any single one of these disciplines leads to a one-sided analysis. Indeed, interdisciplinary approaches involving two or more of them applied to selected research problems have emerged. Examples of scientific conferences which embody such approaches are CHI and the German "Mensch und Computer" Conferences, where in particular the collaboration between disciplines is furthered. Truly interdisciplinary research involving pairs of disciplines, or even triplets or quadruples of these areas, are still few and far between.

At the same time, a number of research universities world wide have risen to the task of providing formal structures in which interdisciplinary teaching and research on these topics can take place. In particular, degree programs have been developed in which faculty from the different areas contribute to teaching undergraduate or – more often – graduate students with the goal of leading the next generation of scientists toward interdisciplinary research. Such degree programs place a large burden on their students, as they are to integrate in their minds the teaching of various different subjects – often with goal of achieving a deeper understanding of the interdisciplinary nature of the subjects than their professors from any one of the contributing subjects might have. In keeping with this challenge, such degree programs are often associated with centers of excellence in research within the respective institutions.

In April, 2003 representatives of a group of German research universities offering degree programs in the areas of **Computational Visualistics** (CV) and **Media Informatics** (MI) (together abbreviated CVMI) met for the first time in Magdeburg, Germany. Their goal is to collaborate in research and research-oriented teaching through the exchange of ideas, information and experience. This volume collects information on their views of their own degree and research programs as a starting point for discussions. The volume also contains examples of interdisciplinary research being carried out in the area.

The CVMI Group has decided to collaborate in a number of areas. Eventually this is to take place in a virtual community, hence this volume presents a number of papers on this topic. In the meantime a web site **www.cvmi.net** with information on the CVMI Group's activities is being built up. The first of these activities are:

- **CVMI Summer School**
  Students at the various institutions are to be given the opportunity to network among one another and also take part in specialized courses offered by faculty at other uni-

versities. Therefore the CVMI group plans to carry out a first Summer School in about August, 2004. The CVMI Summer School 2004 is being organized by Jürgen Friedrich of the University of Bremen.

- **Registry of Graduates**

  The number of graduates in the new degree programs of the CVMI group is small and for the foreseeable future will remain relatively small compared to those of mainstream computer science programs. Graduates can join a virtual community which will provide them with the possibility to interact with one another. The community will also provide and interface for employers to post job offers. The editor is Jürgen Friedrich of the University of Bremen.

- **Collection of Teaching and Research Materials as well as Data**

  One of the challenges of a new interdisciplinary topic as is being addressed by the CVMI group is that specific research compendia as well as teaching materials and data often have to be developed and compiled. This is necessary on the one hand to provide impulses for interdisciplinary research as well as to cater adequately to the interests and needs of the students in the interdisciplinary degree programs.

  The CVMI Group will build up a depository of materials which are to be shared. It will have three sections:

  - Research
  - Teaching

    Course descriptions and teaching materials (typically at the graduate level) used to lead students on to their own research topics

  - Data

    Geometric models and other media created at the institutions involved and which are being given away for free for educational and research use.

  The editor is Ian Pitt of University College Cork.

- **Registry of Degree Programs**

  The degree programs of the research universities involved in CVMI share the common goal of wanting to prepare students for the specific challenges of working with new media by using the methods and tools of computer science with an understanding of the context in which the media will be used. The degree programs being offered today were developed largely independently of one another, and each has its own focus. There is thus the need to inform future employers what students who study in the degree programs offered by the institutions represented in the CVMI Group are actually capable of doing. On the other hand, prospective students need to be aware of this and the individual differences between the programs so that they can choose the one that will best allow them to pursue their own interests. The editor is René Rosenbaum of the University of Rostock.

- **Foundations**
  Interdisciplinary research in Computational Visualistics and Media Informatics raises the question as to the relationship between these two topics and the more traditional topics like computer science, design, psychology, education, political science, sociology, and philosophy. The fundamental question which is raised is whether a theoretical basis can be found which defines the new emergent area. A group being organized by Klaus Sachs-Hombach (Philosophy, University of Magdeburg) is investigating these questions. Initially, the other members of the group are Jana Dittmann (Computer Science, University of Magdeburg), Heidi Schelhowe (Computer Science, University of Bremen), Ulrike Spierling (Design, University of Applied Sciences, Erfurt), and Gerhard Weber (Computer Science, Multimedia Campus Kiel).

The CVMI Group actively seeks communication with scientists and university teachers involved in the areas of computational visualistics and media informatics. The English language has been chosen as the language of communication within the group of scientists so that their thoughts can be shared with the international community at large.

The editors wish to thank all those persons who participated in the Workshop, particularly those who volunteered to coordinate the activities listed above. Thanks also to Mara Mellin for proof-reading the papers in this volume.

Jochen Schneider, Thomas Strothotte, Winfried Marotzki
www.cvmi.net
eMail: info@cvmi.net

Table of Contents

Digital Media Studies & Medieninformatik:
Facts, Questions, and Comments

FRIEDER NAKE

The following provides a revised statement concerning the restructuring of the Bachelor's and Master's degrees offered in Digital Media at the University of Bremen, while considering the potential of these changes for the future of German academia.

Facts

The Computer Science and Math Department at the University of Bremen first offered a Bachelor's of Science in Digital Media during the fall semester of 1999/2000. Six semesters later, the university graduated its first class of students in the summer of 2002. The following October, approximately 20 students were enrolled to begin the four semesters leading to a new Master's of Science in Digital Media.

Currently, a maximum of 40 students can begin the Digital Media Bachelor's degree each year, as both faculty and resources are limited, with expectations that the Master's program will also eventually enroll 40 new students per year.

Although *"Medieninformatik"* remains the preferred term, both *"Digital Media Studies"* and *"Medieninformatik"* are titles used to describe the program in Bremen, with *informatik* clearly denoting the centrality of computer science to the degree. Indeed, the *Gesellschaft für Informatik* or the German Academic Association of Computer Science only recognizes a degree as a computer science degree when fifty percent or more of the necessary courses are part of the computer science curriculum.

Project orientation

Project work remains an essential component in Bremen's computer sciences, with the well-established *Diplom* in *Informatik* featuring a four-semester project, wherein students choose a project lasting from the fifth to the eighth semester. Each professor—working jointly with an assistant, offers one contemporary and research-specific project that generally attracts about 15 to 20 students. Moreover, a full day each week is dedicated to project activities, with additional lectures, seminars, and lab sessions providing potential project alternatives as well as intensive topics, which support project research.

Project results are presented at the July convention, in addition to a written report that specifically defines a given problem or set of problems, subsequent methods applied, related design and implementation decisions, and any relevant technical details. These reports frequently reach 100 pages in length, and can be of considerable quality—at times meeting professional conference standards, and generally involve the development and implementation of a software system.

We feel that projects of this intensity and format are quite unique. When the University of Bremen opened in the fall of 1971, each academic program emphasized the development of the project study, thus taking a bold step forward in university teaching. Although, many departments were unable to sustain the financial burden that accompanies project-oriented curriculum, the computer sciences, are fortunate not only to keep the original university standards of 25 years, but actually expand on them.

However, the situation is somewhat different for the newer digital media Bachelor's and Master's degrees, as their respective six and four-week semester duration prohibit project work that lasts longer than two semesters. Even so, we want to maintain a positive learning experience within the project semesters. Clearly, motivation and communication with students during the project semesters is relatively more dynamic in comparison to standard lectures, seminars, and lab settings. Therefore, both Bachelor's and Master's students must do a *two*-semester project. While the Master's projects take place during the second and third semester—with the first semester dedicated to basic lectures and seminars and the fourth reserved for thesis work, the Bachelor projects are much more flexible—allowing students a greater deal of freedom in arranging their own curriculum, such that a student can conduct their project during any of the semester pairs 3/4, 4/5, or 5/6. A more stable structure is currently under consideration, wherein the first three semesters would cover the fundamental and necessary coursework, while the fourth semester would be spent abroad, and project work, advanced courses, and the Bachelor's report—a conclusion of the project work, would take place during the fifth and sixth semesters. Some faculty members feel that such a change would better clarify curricular planning options for both, students and staff.

Internationalism

As the Bachelor's program requires students to spend one full semester abroad in related departments, the department maintains exchange programs with foreign universities to assist students unable to independently secure an approved position abroad. While abroad, students receive 30 ECTS credit points. Essentially, the students are to gain international experience and expand their current viewpoints on their coursework.

Currently, the exchange programs have been successful and relatively unproblematic in that students have been able to go abroad each year. That said, this may be merely due to the newness of the program, such that a slight increase in student enrolment may prove somewhat more difficult. Specifically, students tend to apply to departments within the USA while unable to afford the notably higher tuition fees within the USA, thus necessitating agreements between universities which allow for fee waiver or minimization. At this point, our computer science department keeps contracts with universities in Aarhus (Denmark), Malmö (Sweden),

Galway (Ireland), Trinity College (Ireland), Buffalo (USA), Indianapolis (USA), Denver (USA, pending), and Bombay (Thailand, pending), with each accepting two or three students per year.

Cooperation

Additionally, students complete an internship at a media-related company of at least 12 weeks—although they are not necessarily consecutive. Generally, students use the time between scheduled classes for this practical part of their program, although not all are registered as full time students. Indeed, many have media-related jobs and re-enter university part-time to increase their theoretical and practical knowledge. The *Medieninformatik* program is essentially a combination of computer science, technical media work, and creative and practical design split into the following course concepts and their specified subjects:

- *Basics* (51 ECTS credit points): mathematics, physics and electronics, algorithms and data structures, programming, digital media
- *Digital Media Technology* (24 points): computer graphics, communication technology, computer networks, video and audio processing, databases, hypermedia, virtual reality
- *Theory and Analysis* (12 points): theory and history of media, semiotics, perception, media culture, social implications, legal and economic issues
- *Design* (32 points): design foundations, typography and layout, photography, animation, 3D design, illustration and visualistics, communication design, interactive communication, dramaturgy, multimedia design
- *Applications* (22 points): media engineering, teaching and learning, electronics, telecooperation, fine arts and culture.

Students must also choose electives worth another 5 points. Their project work, internship, and Bachelor's report add an extra 34 points for a total of 180 points.

Design classes are conducted by the local *Hochschule für Künste*, which offers a sister program in Digital Media with an emphasis on design (as opposed to computer science), with their students then studying introductory algorithms and data structure courses at our university. Discussion is ongoing regarding how independent this course might be relative to the standard computer science syllabus, with some arguing that basic computer science training necessitates covering *all* standard computer science courses, while other argue that formal courses for artists should be different. For example, it is possible to start with images and sound, and transfer to rasters and Fourier series rather smoothly without focusing on proofs.

The bilateral exchange of students between computer science at the university and of design at the Hochschule represents the bare bones of larger innovation, wherein Bremen has consolidated the Digital Media courses of its four public academic institutions: the University, the Hochschule für Künste, the Hochschule Bremen, and the Hochschule Bremerhaven. Thus allowing students to attend courses from all of these institutions up to a maximum number of credit points, ultimately receiving a degree from the institution where initial admittance occurred.

Indeed, this joint program points to the future of German academia, wherein the university and the *Fachhochschule* (professional school)—which remain traditionally separate, will begin to fuse. Typically, the Fachhochschule focuses on practical work in industry and administration, with relatively strict and predefined exam-oriented curriculum. In contrast, university education is a place of liberal and research-oriented education, where motivation, self-determination, and results are emphasized over controlled output and rapid degree completion. Over the last 30 years, this clear separation of goals has changed within many disciplines, indicating the potential for a major revision of the entire third level of education in Germany. Additionally, although most education is still essentially free of charge, if this is threatened, it is likely that Fachhochschule and university may be forced into some new kind of alliance. The Medieninformatik program at Bremen could then be considered an early experiment in this fusion.

Finally, the Master's program is also intended to eventually evolve into a joint program, although details remain unclear. We expect 50% of the 40 graduating Master's students to come from abroad, with a given percentage of Bremen graduates immediately entering graduate school thereafter. Whether these figures can be maintained in the future competition for the best quality of students appears doubtful, as experience with the first generation (of only 20 students) is very mixed.

Reflection

Clearly, the joint program is the most problematic component in the Bremen initiative and only exploration of the details regarding the necessary orders and rules of the study conditions reveals how the established traditions of the participating schools cannot easily be forced under one single roof. My speculation concerning the future of academic study programs in Germany under the auspices of current European leveling tendencies is, that the division between Fachhochschule and University education will gradually disappear, as European trends indicate that this division is unlikely to survive. In fact, given the large numbers of young people now seeking an academic education (some 40% of a single generation), there is no effective way of guiding students through the traditional German research-oriented university education without risking tremendous losses, both on a national and individual level.

The German academic tradition is based on a sound democratic principle—that of virtually no tuition fee, which works only when a small or moderate number of students are enrolled. But when 40% of a generation are enrolled, it is likely that only a much smaller percentage are truly interested in the complicated and complex questions which drive the sciences. A majority of these students are simply not willing to invest five, six, or even ten years of study to truly learn a given subject, but hope to gain quick professional training of university caliber, thus bolstering their chances of success in the demanding, ever-changing, and increasingly competitive job market. Only a small percentage, perhaps one out of five students, actually makes the university the core of their intellectual life during those exciting and unique university years.

Under the changing social and political conditions, the Fachhochschule will eventually be united with the university in a new more American type of university—combining several schools and colleges offering professional training in controlled courses that can guarantee a degree over three or four years of rigorous study. Only a small subset of these students will choose to later enter a Master's program in a related discipline as in the traditional academic education.

Although Bremen—with a difficult albeit liberally structured Bachelor's degree in digital media, could effectively pave the way to these academic fusions, we must remain critical of numerous aspects of this all-in-one academic environment. Currently, students rarely utilize this markedly increased freedom of choice in curriculum as transportation between institutions can be laboriously long and thus, decreases the attractiveness of a given course offered at another university several kilometers away. Is the Internet the answer? Virtualization of classes, e-learning? Maybe. But then, why choose a Bremerhaven course instead of one at MIT?

If the joint study program moves forward successfully—which it will when students can move more freely between institutions—the usual segmented class structure will demand a drastic upheaval, wherein the standard twelve weeks of a normal course, could be replaced by *study days* or six consecutive days packed intensely from 8 a.m. to 6 p.m. This would provide plenty of time for group work, assignments, as well as breaks, such that after a week, students could, in effect, complete an entire course. After which they might take a week or two off before starting up again. Although current conditions do not encourage such revolutionary academic planning, under this new structure, it would be easier to choose classes from a variety of environments while creating a more individualized degree.

Third culture?

Indeed, the topic of digital media is highly suitable for testing within this controversial curricular structure when we consider how it survives under similar institutional stratification: the interwoven histories of fine art, of industrial and graphic design, and of computer technology during the 20th century (Lev Manovich recently offered an argument to this end). We may learn a great deal, if, in our attempt to understand digital media, we study what has come to be called the *Third Culture*, potentially enabling us to create new future-oriented programs in university education. Such programs will, when they emerge, be markedly different from contemporary academia—both in content and form.

If one does not think beyond current economic, bureaucratic, and institutional boundaries, our study programs will and are becoming increasingly stagnant, predictably dull or, at best, effectively standard. What is needed now are a few bold and simple principles upon which to base degrees in digital media such as:

- a drastic reduction of formal lecture hours,
- dramatic increase of practical lab group work,
- replacement of the lecture principle by the authentic narrative presented by enthusiastic learned persons,
- full study days and intense working weeks,
- abolition of the distinction between full time and part time study,
- attractive rooms in a mixed style of science lab, artist's studio, and meeting room where individuals and groups of students occupy their dedicated corners,
- clear and flexible curricula that are open for change and based on simple principles of computability, interactivity, digitality, mediality, and beauty,
- thematic semesters defined by students' homelands, by famous individuals, by design topics, as e.g. the semester of China, or the Babbage, Turing, and Chomsky semester, the semester "On the Road" or "Inside Out" etc.,
- above all: a strong sense and dedication for culture that cannot be expressed in plans but only lived by all those involved, students and staff.

References

Although this overview does not reference specific literature, there is rapidly growing body of exciting books, journals, conferences, and events, which cover the discourse on digital media within sociology, philosophy, fine arts, computer science, and cultural studies. The list below is no means a comprehensive selection and the journal, *Leonardo* is a focal point for much of what is happening in areas of art, science, and technology.

Jay David Bolter: *Writing Space. The Computer, Hypertext, and the History of Writing*. Hillsdale, NJ: Lawrence Erlbaum 1991

Jay David Bolter, Richard Grusin: *Remediation. Understanding New Media*. Cambridge, MA: MIT Press 1999

John Brockman (ed.): *The Third culture: Beyond the Scientific Revolution*. New York: Touchstone 1995

Peter Denning, Robert Metcalfe (eds.): *Beyond Calculation. The Next Fifty Years of Computing*. New York: Springer 1997

Oliver Grau: *Virtual Art. From Illusion to Immersion*. Cambridge, MA: MIT Press 2003

Peter Lunenfeld (ed.): *The digital dialectic. New essays on new media*. Cambridge, MA: MIT Press 1999

Peter Lunenfeld: *Snap to grid. A User's Guide to Digital Arts, Media, and Cultures*. Cambridge, MA: MIT Press 2000

Lev Manovich: *The Language of New Media*. Cambridge, MA: MIT Press 2001

Mihai Nadin: *Anticipation*. Baden: Lars Müller 2003

Randall Packer, Ken Jordan (eds.): *Multimedia: from Wagner to Virtual Reality*. New York: W. W. Norton 2001

Media Informatics at the Technical University of Dresden

RAINER GROH

1 Facts and Figures

The Media Informatics degree was first available at the Technical University of Dresden in 1999, and with ever-increasing enrolment, has established itself at an international as well as nationally recognized programme. The degree emphasizes planning electronic media design in combination with practical knowledge regarding the development of new multimedia systems via the following course focus and specializations:

(1) *The structure and function of complex distributed computer systems and technological multimedia trends*—with specializations in computer and VLSI architectures, networks, transmission techniques, operating and multimedia systems.

(2) *Media types, formats, registration, treatment design of multimedia documents and applications*—with specializations in multimedia technology, media design and computer graphics, identification systems and image processing.

(3) *Information handling, data safety, multimedia publishing*—with specializations in data banks, information and coding theory, multimedia technology.

(4) *Design methods, realization techniques, design tools, test processes, project management for complex distributed multimedia applications*—with specializations in software technology, programming languages and tools, cooperative multimedia applications, and media design and computer graphics.

(5) *Human computer interaction, multimedia and intelligent user interfaces, ergonomics, perception and multimedia psychology, didactics, usability*—with specializations in human computer communication, media design and computer graphics, multimedia engineering, knowledge processing, didactics and computer sciences.

Subjects	Semester:	1	2	3	4	Total
Mathematics		4/2	2/2	3/2	3/2	**20**
Technical Computer Sciences						**6**
Computer Architecture		4/2				
and Organisation						
Practical Computer Sciences						**25**
Algorithms and Data Structures		2/2				
Programming			3/1			
Software Technology				2/2		
Operating Systems				3/2		
Databases					2/2	
Computer Networks					2/2	
Media Engineering						**14**
Introduction						
Multimedia Engineering		2/2				
Basics of Design			2/1			
Introduction to Media Design					2/1	
Communication Ergonomics			2/0			
and Media Psychology						
Didactic Electronic Media				2/0		
Theoretical Computer Sciences						**12**
Basics of Logic		2/1				
Basics of Theoretical						
Computer Sciences			2/1	2/1		
Information and Coding Theory			2/1			
Practical Training						**5**
Programming			1			
Software Technology					2	
Media Design					2	
Electives				3	3	**6**
Total		**23**	**20**	**22**	**23**	**88**

Diploma Courses

Subjects Semester:	5/6	7/8	9
Specialization (1)	12		
Practical Training (1)	4		
Specialization (a)	8		
Specialization (b)		8	
Practical Training (a or b)		4	
Consolidation Field		12	
Proseminar	2		
Main Seminar		2	
Major Paper		8	
Electives	7	7	
General Skills	2		
Foreign Language Training		4	
General Studies	4	4	
Total	**43**	**41**	**Diploma**

Media Informatic Enrolment Patterns per Winter Semester

1999/2000: **80** (students)

2000/2001: **370**

2001/2002: **274**

2002/2003: **435**

References

Meißner, Klaus: Draft of the course of studies at the Faculty of Informatics at the TU Dresden, 1999

Rules of Examination and Studies, 1999

2 Media Informatics in Dresden: Developing Design Competence

Currently taught at a technical school, the required design courses form a relatively small percentage of coursework for the Media Informatics Degree, as they lay outside of the spectrum of traditional subjects taught within the computer science department.

A trivial solution:

Design course could be effectively taught as a compressed version of classic design courses, wherein topics such as layout, composition, and colour theory could be systematically covered in small and compact units. This "patchwork" approach would naturally remain somewhat independent from the traditional courses. Indeed, all technical innovations must initiate aesthetic (or cultural) innovations, such that these design course are—in a sense, derivative of primary research and learning processes.

Specifications

Clearly, Media Informatics does not follow typified design degrees, as it relies heavily on much of the computer sciences while maintaining its own necessary special skills:

1. *Managing complex development processes,* wherein the student learns to effectively organize interdisciplinary teams of specialists.
2. *Solving aesthetic problems via functional structure analysis,* wherein computer science initiates the design process as functional structure is frequently neglected within a multitude of design approaches.
3. *Development of a basic understanding of art and design,* wherein all students—not only artistically talented ones, receive a general education in these areas in parallel with applications in software, ergonomics, and logic of use.

A student who learns to effectively integrate these above skills will graduate with the ability to define his or her role in a given design process in cooperation with other design specialists—whether cameramen, graphic designers, or artists. This solution optimally fuses computer science and design, such that the image becomes the 'venue', as seen in the following:

- All complex technical systems rely on images (whether a medical robot or game).
- Software and related tools are developed for effective use within our essentially visual information world, such that mathematics must incorporate aspects of image and shape.
- Various aspects of interaction, communication and dialogue have always remained central themes within art itself.

Coursework must then be properly subdivided into units:

Project Work

Because design courses fulfil portions of the technical degree requirements, student pro-jects—as defined by faculty research, must also incorporate a suitable level of design-oriented work.

Potential project topics are listed below.

- Computer based training
- Navigation systems
- Interactive user interfaces (expert systems, medical robotics, games, etc.)
- Interfaces for the disabled or geriatric population
- Multimedia storytelling.

Specialized theory

Theory emphasizes analysis and synthesis with consideration for cultural processes and precedents in terms of principles and methods, as can be seen in the following list of topics:

- History of interaction,
- History of images,
- Typology of interfaces,
- Logic of use,
- Aesthetics and semiotics,
- Typology of multimedia scenarios and
- Mathematics and images.

The Basics

Although a media informatics student does not necessarily need an in-depth understanding of graphic/interface design, they must understand the basic aesthetic aspects of their product in order to properly integrate their work with other members.

- Typography and colour
- Doctrines of arrangement and composition
- Layout (static and dynamic)
- Multimedia tools
- Functional elements of graphical user interfaces (buttons, icons, pictographs etc.)
- Image Boundaries (frames, view-finder, format)

As teaching generally maintains a corresponding field of research, two currently relevant is-sues to cover are:

- How to support the navigation of 3D- and 2D-Images in virtual spaces
- How adaptive or pre-determined a given interface should be

Final comment

Clearly, aesthetically-geared courses within our Media Informatics Degree, must offer a new fusion of design and theory, such that the 'trivial solution' is unsuitable as it is merely additive. The media informatics student must become a creator of both rich as well as functional products. Rich, because they can take on several shapes, because they are 'open'. As a trained computer scientist they are able to envision the functional structure of the product from the beginning. Gone are the days when the designer was sent in the last phase of product development to make things look nice.

Media Informatics at the University of Munich

HEINRICH HUSSMANN

1 Introduction

Founded in 1472, with over 45000 students today, the University of Munich (Ludwig-Maximilians-Universität) is one of the largest and oldest universities in Germany. Currently the university offers 123 different degree programmes of which only Computer Science (Informatics) is part of the engineering discipline. Consequently, the computer science degree focuses heavily on building bridges between computer science and other disciplines and has recently led to the introduction of a new, multi-disciplinary study programme called "Medieninformatik" (Media Informatics). The following briefly overviews the programme and experiences of the first students enrolled in the Media Informatics programme during the 2001/2002 winter term.

2 Organisation of the Study Programme

Currently, the Media Informatics programme reflects the requirements necessary to fulfil a traditional German "diploma" degree programme, although there is discussion of developing the degree to better follow the more internationally recognised Bachelor and Master degree.

Because of the novelty of the programme and because Media Informatics demands more specialised hardware and software relative to traditional Computer Science, admission into the programme is currently limited to 70 students per year, and is based on high-school exam grades ("numerus clauses").

Although Media Informatics is run by the Computer Science department, it is a multi-disciplinary degree, as both the Institute for Communication Sciences and the School of Business are heavily involved in the programme, with planned extensions to other departments underway. Indeed, Media Informatics students must choose an area of specialisation within the *application area*: either *media research* (provided by the Communication Sciences group) or *media economics* (provided by the Business Administration group). Instead of diffusing the focus to include "a little bit of everything", we emphasise specialisation in only one area outside Computer Science, thus exceeding the traditional Computer Science minor and allowing for a solid education in an area outside of informatics.

Following the German diploma degree, the curriculum begins with two years of strictly structured basic studies, which end in intensive final exams. After successful completion, the much more liberal advanced studies phase can commence. In general, the curriculum consists of four parts:

- Computer Science
- Mathematics (slightly less emphasised relative to the Computer Sciences)
- Media-oriented technology, in particular multimedia technology
- Application area (media research of media economics)

The course focus within these areas is roughly as follows:

	Computer Science	Mathematics	Media Technology	Application Area
Basic studies	40 %	20 %	15 %	25 %
Advanced studies	40 %	0 %	40 %	20 %

In addition to the traditional courses, the Media Informatics degree contains a number of seminars and practical projects. In the final phase of their studies, students are expected to design and present a full-scale application project (ideally in co-operation with industry). Lastly, the diploma thesis is delivered and may also comprise a significant amount of practical work.

3   First Experiences

The question students or prospective students most frequently ask is: *What is the difference between Computer Science and Media Informatics?* Our answer at the University of Munich is somewhat different from other related programmes. Typically, media informatics programmes expect students to focus on many different disciplines, thus pre-empting the possibility of developing in depth knowledge in any one of these disciplines. In contrast, we emphasise the intensive study of one secondary scientific discipline, thus allowing students to explore two separate disciplines and how dissimilar their scientific languages and disciplinary paradigms can be. Consequently, students learn to work in that area which lies between radically different disciplines. Admittedly, this experience can be frustrating, but it aptly mirrors the current state of media sciences. To better assist students in bridging the interdisciplinary gap, we are currently developing seminars and lectures that encompass several disciplines, including a seminar series on "economy of innovative Internet services" planned for winter 2003.

4   Research Programme

The Munich concept of Media Informatics is more than just a degree, as we are planning to develop focused research that addresses interdisciplinary topics. As a first step in this direction, a research project on "Internet economy" is planned for the end of 2003 with participation from the Computer Science department, as well as the social sciences and economics. Further interdisciplinary contacts and ideas for collaborations are welcome.

Additionally, a Media Informatics research group is currently planning to investigate the following potential issues:

1. *Model based development of multimedia applications and Web services*: In co-operation with other disciplines, this is an approach that relies mainly on an abstract, diagrammatic model of services prior to implementation. This should provide both greater platform independence for development as well as multidisciplinary analyses of service.

2. *Innovative user interfaces for Ubiquitous Computing*: tangible, physical user interfaces will be studied as a tool for easy access to "disappearing" computer applications.

3. *Application support for "Quality of Service"*: Based on results from recent European-funded research projects, a technology will be provided which enables legacy applications and new services built with simple state-of-the-art Web authoring technologies to get access to advanced resource reservation schemes available in an Internet of next generation.

4. *Lightweight multimedia support for teaching*: Simple forms of creating multimedia teaching material will be studied, which avoid the overhead of media production and instead can be produced as a side-product of the normal provision of course materials (e.g. slides).

5 Conclusion

The Media Informatics programme at the University of Munich differs from other such programmes in its clear multidisciplinary structure, which comprises clear and extensive commitments within other departments besides Computer Science. Moreover, our specific approach chooses not to focus on the basics of a large number of disciplines, but rather to intensively educate students in two drastically different fields. Currently, the necessary degree courses are available, with related interdisciplinary research projects now commencing, all of which will be closely interconnected to the actual Media Informatics Programme.

New Degree Programmes at Augsburg University: Bachelor's/Masters for "Informatics and Multimedia"

ELISABETH ANDRÉ

The Bachelor's programme for "Informatics and Multimedia" was conceived in October 2002 by the Institute for Informatics at Augsburg University in order to form a bridge between the natural and social sciences.

Programme Objectives

The Bachelor's programme is designed to more effectively satisfy the growing industrial demand within German IT for highly skilled media specialists with a proper background in the computer sciences. The programme prepares students for emerging novel technological challenges within computer sciences, telecommunications and media industries. Consequently, graduates are educated within various areas of the media sector including:

- the introduction and maintenance of multimedia systems
- the design, implementation, and evaluation of multimedia applications and user interfaces
- the technical supervision of multimedia productions

We specifically provide the basic methods and skills necessary to informatics without requiring an early specialization, thus enabling students to better respond to rapid industry developments.

The programme distinguishes itself from competing programmes via markedly emphasizing e-learning issues. The programme not only teaches students the technical skills necessary to the design and implementation of successful multimedia applications, but also how this media can be applied in educationally beneficial manners.

Related Institutions and Departments

Although a majority of courses are taught by the Institute for Informatics, the Department for Mathematics contributes basic courses on mathematics, while the Philosophical and Socio-Scientific Faculty contribute to a more rounded and interdisciplinary education. Moreover, the degree is complemented by design courses offered by external media specialists

Enrolment

Sixty four first-year students enrolled to comprise 28% of all first-year informatics students. Altogether around 100 students were enrolled for the programme.

Programme Structure

The main difference between the new Bachelor's programme and the classical Applied Informatics diploma programme is an increased emphasis regarding multimedia issues as well as a more interdisciplinary orientation. Thus, the programme consists of four basic building blocks:

- Theoretical Foundations of Computer Science and Mathematics
- Practical Informatics
- Multimedia
- Media Pedagogy and Communication Sciences

The multimedia block of the programme includes a mandatory elementary multimedia course. In addition, students must successfully complete courses from at least two of the following four categories:

- *Multimedia Foundations*
  Multimedia Databases, Multimedia Retrieval, Multimedia Analysis, Multimedia Authoring, Software Engineering for Multimedia etc.

- *System-oriented Aspects of Multimedia*
  Data Compression, Optical Storage Media, Multimedia Networks, Multimedia Signal Processing etc.

- *Multimedia Man-Machine Communication*
  Interaction Techniques, Multimedia Dialog Systems, Agent-based Multimedia Interaction, Multimedia User and Discourse Modelling etc.

- *Multimedia Applications*
  Information Systems, Game Programming, Tutoring Applications, Multimedia Edutainment etc.

Examples of courses offered during 2002/2003 include: Multimedia Analysis (Multimedia Foundations); Introduction to Multimedia Signal Processing (System-Oriented Aspects of Multimedia); Animated Interface Agents (Multimedia Man-Machine Communication), Computer Music (Multimedia Applications); and Computer Game Programming (Multimedia Applications).

Lectures on multimedia issues are complemented by seminars and practical teamwork. Like the diploma students, Bachelor's students must conduct a software project in cooperation with a company willing to serve as a fictitious customer. Specialized multimedia projects are also offered. For example, in winter 2002, students developed an augmented reality application for the City of Augsburg. In addition to informatics courses, students must complete courses in the areas "Media and Communication" and "Media Pedagogy" offered by the Philosophical and Socio-Scientific Departments within the university.

The Research Environment at Augsburg University

From the beginning, the Institute for Informatics focused heavily on multimedia in planning for the HTO extension project, which was funded by a 10 Million Euro grant from the Bavarian government. Two of four new chair positions were devoted to multimedia: (1) the chair for "Multimedia Concepts and its Applications" and (2) the chair for "Software Techniques for Multimedia Applications" (currently occupied). In addition, related multimedia issues are represented by the chair for "Data Bases and Information Systems" and the chair for "System-oriented Informatics".

Currently, the programme is largely conducted within the lab for Multimedia Concepts and their Applications, which focuses on multimedia interfaces, conversational agents, user modelling, and user motion tracking. In order to more effectively create and optimise human-computer interactions, the lab follows a highly interdisciplinary approach, involving not only computer scientists, but also designers, electrical-engineers, and cognitive scientists. Ongoing research consists of the following projects:

- *Natural Interaction With Virtual Characters*
  In order to explore new forms of communication between humans and virtual actors, we are currently designing an unobtrusive user tracking system. A team of virtual characters is displayed on a projection wall, which react to the user's motion by means of gestures, mimics and speech (see Fig. 1). The behaviour of the virtual actors is controlled by several autonomous reactive planning modules. The general idea here is not to specify the characters' behaviour to the last detail, but give them instructions that they may refine and work out while interacting with the user during the actual presentation.

- *Concept Learning in 3D Environments*
  In this project, we examine how a culturally different organization of reality can be educationally employed using intelligent interface agents. Based on empirical findings of cross-linguistics studies, we realized a computational model of concept formation in the spatial domain that relies on visual and linguistic input. Virtual, anthropomorphic agents autonomously explore their complex 3D environment, sensing it with a visual sensor while obtaining linguistic input from an interlocutor. This input describes the current situations (e.g. "the animal is in front of the house"). Connecting linguistic competence and sensory abilities, the agents are able to then create the necessary dis-criminative features in self-organization and selection processes.

- *Affective Feedback Loops in Man-Machine Communication*
  A new generate-and-sense model continuously analyses the user's physiological feedback and responds to it during user interaction. The state of human emotion is statistically modelled and predicted by analysing the sensed physiological signals including electromyogram (EMG), blood volume pressure and skin conductivity. As a first application scenario a music player selects music, thus setting acoustical environments (e.g., treble/base balance and sound pressure level at each channel) based on the user's physiological feedback.

Figure 1: Natural Interaction with Virtual Characters

The Bachelor's programme is integrated with both basic and applied research projects within our lab. Indeed, the mandatory multimedia projects are inspired by the lab's research objectives. In addition, students are able to assist or conduct research in our lab as student researchers.

The programme also strongly profits from international cooperation with institutions and corporations such as the German Research Center for Artificial Intelligence (DFKI), Mitre (US), the Fraunhofer Institute for Computer Graphics Darmstadt, the Vienna University of Technology, Bielefeld University, Honda, and Siemens AG.

Future Plans

The notable success of the bachelor's programme has led to the subsequent design of a complementary Master's program, intended for autumn 2003. While the Bachelor's programme emphasizes the development of practical skills, the Master's programme will be characterized by a stronger integration of research and teaching.

Virtual Communities:
Cooperation and Awareness Support

WOLFGANG PRINZ

Introduction

This paper describes two approaches to support cooperation in combination with presence and task awareness in virtual communities. The first system is the Social Web Cockpit, an assistant that supports users while traversing the World Wide Web. The cockpit provides awareness and supports collaboration, notification of interesting Web pages, collaborative construction of community knowledge, and the development of a community vocabulary. The cockpit aims at turning the World Wide Web from an interaction medium into a cooperation tool, for the active support and self-organization of virtual communities. The cockpit is a result from our "Social Web Research Program" at Fraunhofer-FIT which aims to explore and demonstrate how we can turn information environments into rich communication and interaction environments [3].

The second system is an awareness environment that offers different means for the presentation of activity information and the creation of topic based chance encounters in a cooperative environment. This includes a populated 3D environment for an overview on team activities, as well as 2D visualizations that are integrated in the application context.

There have been several approaches to support knowledge sharing in communities: shared workspaces, recommender systems, annotation and rating systems, or shared ontologies. They all suffer from an imbalance of effort versus benefit from the individual's point of view. The World Wide Web, or Web for short, is the place and medium where both systems offer their services. They turn Web sites into meeting places where visitors may become aware of each other, open communication channels, and exchange information and knowledge with each other or with experts. Usually people visit a Web site in search of some information. So there is some chance that its visitors may have overlapping interests, if the site matches their expectations, backgrounds, or motivations. These people might well profit from each other's knowledge by sharing opinions, experiences or advice. Some visitors might enter long-term relationships – if only they became aware of each other. Basic functions for this requirement are provided by systems such as CoBrow [9] or ThirdVoice [11].

A community of users should further be enabled to structure and filter the Web according to their needs, based on opinions, recommendations, and personal relations. For example, visitors may enrich the Web site with their knowledge by recommending Web pages and related links, or by annotating and discussing them. People may also add their own documents in shared workspaces, they may highlight key phrases and begin to reach a common understanding by involving new concepts. These concepts should be automatically cross-referenced with the site and related Web pages to support content-based navigation. Search facilities should take into account concepts and collaborative ratings. Visitors may select pages from the site to be monitored for changes that will be indicated upon their next visit.

We expect that communities that are supported with such services may become very attractive because they offer the chance to meet again, to see what is new, and to inspect the growing number of contributions by its members. Such an assistant can be compared with a cooperatively developed and mobile portal that dynamically evolves through use within a community.

Cockpit Functionality

In this section the cockpit is presented from a user's perspective. We will first present an overview followed by a subsection presenting the cockpit functions that support awareness. A further subsection describes the services for collaborative collection of information.

Overview

Communities, in the context of the cockpit, are groups of people sharing a common interest or task and interacting electronically. The people are called members of a community. Each community has a name and owns a collection of information collaboratively acquired and shared by its members.

The cockpit provides simple but effective means for the creation of communities and the management of community membership. It is realised as a small window that occupies only a little space on the computer screen (see figure 1); all actions and controls can be dragged out in separate tiny windows. Therefore, most users don't need to reorganize their desktop when using the cockpit. The standard configuration consists of a browser window and the cockpit window on the screen.

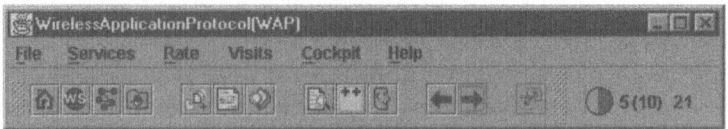

Figure 1. User interface of the Social Web Cockpit.

Whenever a Web page is visited that belongs to a community where the user is a member, the tool automatically notifies the user of the name of the community and of other visitors to the page. If the cockpit window is iconified, then the user gets informed through changes in the symbolic representation. This is a second type of working configuration with minimal desktop space requirements but still a basic amount of awareness.

A third working configuration (cockpit window and two browser windows) appears when the user calls a function that is executed by one of the component systems of the cockpit. For example, if a Web page which the user wants to add to the pool of documents of a community appears in the browser window and the user presses the upload button in the cockpit, then a second browser window with a BSCW [1] template is opened to enter name and description details.

Awareness Services

The cockpit is a companion for the World Wide Web. When visiting Web sites, users get informed about the presence of others and get notified about some characteristics of the Web site. In contrast to other tools with similar functionality, the cockpit offers all services at all Web sites.

For the following we assume, that a Web page currently visited belongs to a community named 'Wireless Application Protocol (WAP)'. We assume also, that the user is a member of this community. First, the user gets informed, that this Web page belongs to this community. The name is shown in the title bar of the cockpit window or in the iconified window of the cockpit.

Graphical symbols indicate the presence of others. Rightmost in the cockpit's window (see figure 1) the number of persons in the community and their maximum number (number of members) as well as the number of cockpit users is shown. In our case there are 5 of 10 users visiting Web pages of this community and 21 persons are currently using the cockpit.

Each community has one distinguished member, the expert, by default its creator. For Web sites or pages, however, there may be experts too. The presence of an expert for the Web site or the community is directly indicated, and if the expert is present the cockpit users can call and communicate with her/him. As an example tool for communication with experts we are currently using Netmeeting, i.e. a function is offered that is comparable with a call center where one can get in touch with a specialist for a Web site.

The median of the collaborative rating of the currently visited Web page is presented in the cockpits user interface by a symbolic representation. For the rating there are five symbols representing the values poor, passable, fair, good, and excellent. The indication of the rating is a further important awareness function, i.e. users are informed at a glance about the quality of the Web page as assessed by members of the community.

Services for the Cooperative Collection of Information

Although the use of the Internet and the World Wide Web is widespread, not all users have their own Web site. As a solution to this problem, the cockpit offers so-called shared workspaces. For each community there exists an associated shared workspace which is named "documents". Documents of any type can be put into this workspace. In this way, community members are enabled to create a collection of common documents. An even more important shared workspace of each community is named "link collection". This workspace contains only links to Web pages, collected collaboratively by the members of the community. Both collections are realized as BSCW shared workspaces and can be accessed through buttons in the user interface of the cockpit. The content of the collections is shown in an extra browser window. These collections enable members of communities to present their own documents on the Web without having to be able to create Web documents.

The two shared workspaces for each community differ in the type of the collected documents. Documents in general cannot be analyzed by computers. The link collection contains links to Web pages or the Web pages themselves. They are all written in HTML or XML format. This document format can be analyzed by computers, at least to a certain extent. This capability is especially used for the ConceptIndex service of the cockpit. Before we describe this service we will present the function for rating Web pages.

All documents in a community can be rated using the corresponding cockpit function. There are five discrete values available: poor, passable, fair, good and excellent. Note, that the mode of this function is also collaborative, i.e. a common rating is calculated as the median of all ratings. Each member of a community can make only one rating. The median is directly shown in the user interface of the cockpit. However, individual ratings can also be inspected, and the documents of the shared workspaces can be sorted according to the rating values. This function enables groups to develop a common estimation of information. Imagine, for example, a team of co-located persons collecting information for a survey of the state of the art of WAP.

For a community, it is not sufficient to collaboratively collect documents; it is also necessary to reach a common understanding. The ConceptIndex [12] service of the cockpit enables members to create their own vocabulary. Each vocabulary belongs to the Web pages in the link collection of a community. A vocabulary consists of concepts, i.e. words and phrases, which are important and characteristic for these Web pages. Adding a concept to a vocabulary is like dragging a marker over text on a paper document. The user selects the word or phrase with the mouse and chooses to add this concept to the vocabulary. In addition, the new concept can stand in different relations to other concepts: synonym, sub-concept, enclosing concept.

The vocabulary of a community can be used during browsing the Web: when a Web page is visited all matching concepts of the vocabulary are superimposed with a special color to highlight them. This feature provides a first estimate of whether a Web page is relevant for a community and worth collecting. Note that ConceptIndex uses word stemming of words as well as exact matching for the matching of concepts to words in documents.

The ConceptIndex service maintains an index with cross-references of the concepts in the vocabulary to the Web pages in the link collection of a community. This cross-reference enables users to navigate in the link collection using the concepts. The cross-reference is automatically updated when a concept is added, modified, or removed.

TOWER

The TOWER system [7] aims at bringing the wealth of clues and information that create awareness and cohesion in co-located teams to the world of virtual teams and to present them in a Theatre of Work. This information is important for the mutual orientation in cooperative work processes but also for the social interaction. Organisations are more and more restructured around virtual teams. Thus 'they loose opportunities for innovation through the causal sharing of knowledge and learning induced by physical proximity' [10] or as Prusak [8] describes this phenomenon vividly: 'If the water cooler was a font of useful knowledge in the traditional firm, what constitutes a virtual one?'

TOWER aims at supporting group awareness and chance encounters through a 3D environment that is at the heart of the Theatre of Work. Avatars and symbolic actions represent users and their current actions on shared objects while using a groupware application. Avatars of users who work in a similar context appear spatially close in the 3D environment. The Avatars perform symbolic actions that illustrate events in an information space, episodes of interaction or non-verbal behaviour.

We believe that the provision of such a service is vital for the successful cooperation and knowledge sharing within distributed teams that use the WWW and other Internet applications as the preliminary cooperation platform.

The TOWER system is composed of a number of interworking components. Figure 2 illustrates the overall TOWER architecture.

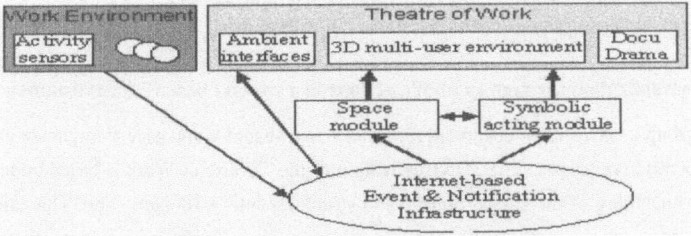

Figure 2. Illustration of the TOWER architecture.

It consists of:

• A number of different activity sensors that capture and recognise user activities in a real and virtual work environment and that submit appropriate events.

- An Internet-based event & notification infrastructure that receives events and forwards these events to interested and authorised users.
- A space module that dynamically creates 3D spaces from virtual information environments (e.g., shared information workspaces such as Lotus Notes) and that adopts existing spaces to the actual usage and work behaviour of the users that populate these spaces.
- A symbolic acting module that transforms event notifications about user actions into symbolic actions, i.e. animated gestures of the avatars that represent users and their activities in the environment.
- A 3D multi-user environment that interoperates with the symbolic acting and space module for visualisation and interaction.
- The 3D visualisation is complemented by ambient interfaces integrated into the physical workplace providing activity visualisation beyond the standard desktop.
- A DocuDrama component that transforms sequences of event notifications and history information into a narrative of the past cooperative activities.

The primary goal of TOWER is the presentation of activities in a cooperative environment through symbolic acting in the Theatre of Work. This requires an event and notification infrastructure that is capable of recognising and sensoring user activities on shared objects or in a shared environment [6]. TOWER includes an infrastructure that is fully integrated with the Internet. This infrastructure provides a number of sensors that can be integrated with user applications using Internet protocols such as HTTP, which are available in almost all standard application nowadays. In addition, agent-like sensors are realised that observe information sources and the population of information by users. All sensors submit events that encapsulate activity information to the infrastructure.

Tasks of the infrastructure are to store, aggregate, and forward the activity information to applications that have registered interest in the appropriate information. For the interaction with other applications push and pull methods are realised. Methods are developed to ensure restricted access to activity information access rights, and to provide reciprocity for ensuring transparency between producers and consumers of information.

Activity visualization through symbolic actions in a context based 3D environment

Often a group uses a shared document repository as a shared workspace to organize and support cooperation processes. The 3D visualization of the Theatre of Work is based upon a context based mapping of the shared objects and structures into a 3D landscape. This landscape contains representations of shared working objects such as documents, folders, distribution lists, calendars, etc. This representation can be very detailed: in this case each shared document is represented by one object in the 3D world. Or, it can be more abstract: in this case only folder structures or aggregations of shared objects are represented.

The construction of such a world can be done automatically using the space module. This module allows users to select the type of objects that shall be represented as well as the grouping and arrangement of objects based on their semantics. I.e. objects can be grouped based on their location in a shared folder, or on other attributes such as key words, owner, etc. The representation may include objects from different applications, e.g. calendar, database, shared workspace, file systems, distribution lists. Thus, the 3D landscape combines the material from different cooperation tools, reflecting the fact that users organize their cooperative work with more than a single tool. The openness of the ENI-server and the provision of simple cgi-interfaces contribute to the goal of TOWER to provide an awareness environment that integrates and combines different applications and interaction styles.

The same cooperation environment can be represented by different landscape designs that show different levels of detail or different contextualization of the shared objects. Figures 3 and 4 show examples of abstract and detailed worlds.

Figure 3. An abstract overview world showing different project contexts

The TOWER world is populated with avatars that represent users and their actions in a symbolic way [5]. This is realized by automatically moving avatars to places in the 3D world that correspond to the working context or the document the user is currently working on. Symbolic gestures of the avatar represent the last action of the user. For example, a read operation is visualized by an avatar reading a newspaper, while an avatar that is typing on a large typewriter indicates a write operation. The automatic placement of the avatar and the symbolic actions are controlled by the space and symbolic acting module of the TOWER system. The avatars are moved automatically through the 3D world based on the user actions on the represented shared material. I.e. the 3D world is primarily intended for visualization but not for navigation. Users do not need to navigate through the 3D world to access documents.

Activities of team members are represented in TOWER only when they are working in the shared environment or when they perform activities in a public space. This distinguishes the TOWER approach from video based media spaces [4], where users are visible independently of their current working context.

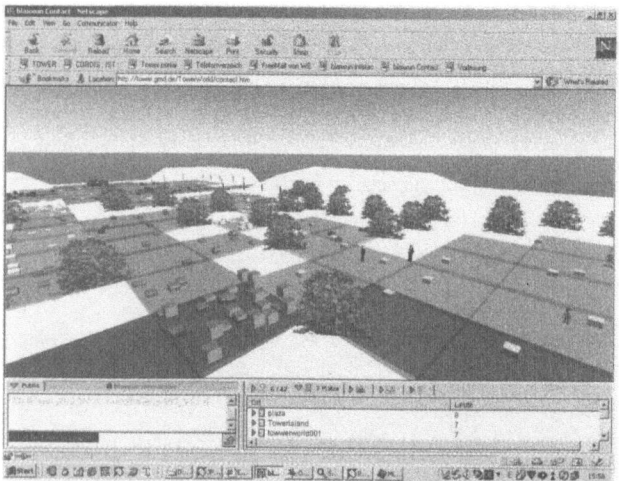

Figure 4. A detailed TOWER world representing individual documents

The exaggerated presentation of user activities by symbolic actions provides a good over-view on the activities in a world and the overall situation, also from a distance. User can eas-ily recognize which documents, tasks, or colleagues currently perform related processes. Us-ers whose avatars are close to each other in the TOWER world are also working in a similar working context.

Communication channels such as audio or chat are provided to enable a spontaneous con-versation. Thus the TOWER world serves as a chance encounter and context based meeting space that facilitates coincidental meetings.

For peripheral awareness on user activities the TOWER world is projected or displayed in the users' office environment. Alternatively it can also be included as an extension in the us-ers' web browser (Internet-Explorer only). Figure 5 shows the TOWER world as part of a web browser. In this scenario the user is currently working with a cooperative document man-agement system that stores project documents organized in different work packages. The 3D world represents the different work packages by different boxes. While users navigate through the document store, they see the current location of their own avatar and the avatars of other users in the 3D window. Thus they see immediately if they are working "close" to other users.

Users can employ camera agents for a guided tour through the TOWER world. This can include all places where the user has been active recently, all places where other users are currently active or a predefined list of places.

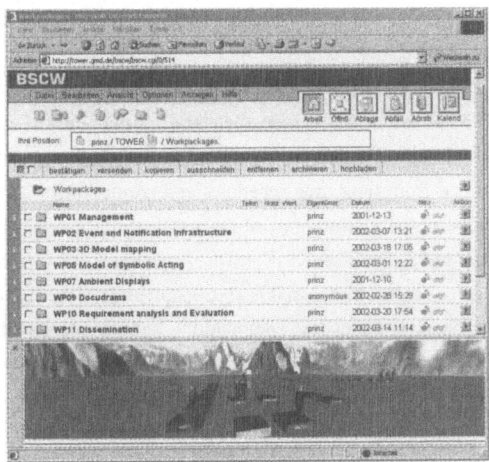

Figure 5: TOWER World as integral part of the web browser

Conclusion

Berners-Lee's [2] vision for the World Wide Web was the support of cooperation through shared knowledge. This requires the development of Web-based cooperation support tools that enable a social and qualitative orientation within a community and its information base. The cockpit integrates different systems to support these aspects. Social orientation is supported by the combination of an awareness service with rating and recommendation services. This supports the collaborative construction of a shared terminology which enables a qualitative orientation.

The cockpit facilitates new forms of support for virtual communities. So far most systems provide a central community site that needs to be visited by the users to get in touch with the community. In contrast the cockpit offers a community service to its users at any place in the Web. It recognises community relevant places, points the user to other community members and supports the structuring, extension, and rating of community-relevant information. It turns the Web from an information medium into a cooperation tool, for the active support and self-organisation of communities. For further integration of the cockpit functionality into the users working tools, its functionalities are currently integrated as a new toolbar into the Internet Explorer.

The cockpit functionalities are augmented by the TOWER approach that opens new workplaces which enable people to benefit from currently available network technology for the development of new working situations for distributed teams. Thus, the limitations of working condition of non-collocated groups or teams can be overcome. Teamwork depends deeply on the opportunity of its members to have immediate occasions for social contact. Social contacts are relevant for both the smooth progress of cooperative work as well as for the motivation and well being of the individuals. Currently distributed team work suffers from the lack of occasions for face-to-face social contacts.

With its ability to manage temporal discontinuities and replay past situations and the past course of work, TOWER can help team members and communities to understand the causes of the current situation despite temporal absence and to catch up to the current situation. Thus team members are freed from tight time schedules and are no longer handicapped in case of absences. Tower supports the maintenance of co-presence in the team and the continuity of work despite temporal discontinuities.

The usage of systems such as the Social Web Cockpit and TOWER increase the likeliness of synergy effects to occur in teams and communities, and may contribute to improved team cohesion. The perception of co-presence may effect the quality of the work with respect to the quality of the outcome. It will improve the working atmosphere by the reduction of planning, synchronisation, and coordination efforts. It will avoid or at least reduce the feeling of isolation of distributed communities and will contribute to orientation in both the social and the task related environment.

Literature

1. Appelt, W. *WWW Based Collaboration with the BSCW System*. in *SOFSEM'99*. 1999. Milovy, Czech Republic: Springer Lecture Notes in Computer Science 1725.
2. Berners-Lee, T. and M. Fischetti, *Weaving the Web*. 1999, New York: Harper Collins Publishers.
3. Hoschka, P., W. Prinz, and U. Pankoke-Babatz, *Der Computer als soziales Medium*, in *CSCW-Kompendium*, Schwabe, Streitz, and Unland, Editors. 2001, Springer: Berlin, Heidelberg, New York. p. 276-285.
4. Lee, A., A. Girgensohn, and K. Schlueter. *NYNEX Portholes: Initial User Reactions and Redesign Implications*. in *Group'97 Conference*. 1997. Phoenix, AZ: ACM Press.
5. McGrath, A., *The Forum*. ACM SIGGROUP Bulletin, 1998. **19**(3): p. 21-24.
6. Prinz, W. *NESSIE: An Awareness Environment for Cooperative Settings*. in *ECSCW'99: Sixth Conference on Computer Supported Cooperative Work*. 1999. Copenhagen: Kluwer Academic Publishers.
7. Prinz, W., et al., *Presenting activity information in an inhabited information space*, in *Inhabited Information Spaces*, D. Snowdon, Editor. 2003, Springer.
8. Prussak, L., *Knowledge in Organizations*. 1997, Oxford: Butterworth-Heinemann.
9. Siedler, G., A. Scott, and H. Wolf. *Collaborative Browsing in the World Wide Web*. in *JENC8: 8th Joint European Networking Conference*. 1997. Edinburgh.
10. Swan, J., et al., *Knowledge management and innovation: networks and networking*. Journal of Knowledge Management, 1999. **3**(4): p. 262-275.

11.   Third Voice, *Third Voice*. 1999: ThirdVoice.com.
12.   Voss, A., K. Nakata, and M. Juhnke. *Concept Indexing*. in *GROUP'99: International ACM SIGGROUP Conference on Supporting Group Work*. 1999. Phoenix, AZ: ACM Press.

Virtual Institutes: Between Immersion and Communication

KLAUS SACHS-HOMBACH, JÖRG R.J. SCHIRRA, JOCHEN SCHNEIDER

1 Three Uses of the Expression 'Virtual'

Both "virtual reality" (VR) and "virtual community" use the word "virtual" to convey different meanings. A VR is a depiction or, more generally speaking, a sensory representation of reality that allows the user – mainly via interaction – to experience various features of reality without actually being in contact with the reality depicted. Hence, any interactive depiction, which allows for a certain degree of sensory-motor immersion, is known as virtual reality (Heim 1998, 6f). Although the user rarely (if ever) doubts the difference between a given VR and what it represents—because reality is both more unpredictable and complex than any virtual depiction, VR has the advantage of being controlled and safe in a way that their "real" counterparts can never guarantee.

In contrast, virtual communities—although employing aspects of VR—are indeed "real" communities, as they necessarily include real people and their subsequent interactions. Clearly, without real agents, intentions, and interactions, there is nothing more than a mere simulation of a community. What, then, is the difference between virtual communities and real communities? The most obvious distinction is mediation via computer-based devices, although an internet-based video conference would never be considered a virtual conference. Thus, computerized mediation alone is insufficient grounds for defining a community interaction as a virtual one. We would like to suggest that a community is properly characterized by the term "virtual" only if (a) the mediating devices allow the participating persons to disguise their identities, and if (b) other participants are aware of this possibility. Essentially, a virtual community allows participants to mask their real names, personal attributes, and other identifying traits connected to their actual person, in exchange for a user name and identity that they created and can choose to share with members of the virtual community.

A virtual *institute* combines the concepts of VR and virtual communities: with no physical building or meeting place and real "overt" members, the institute can potentially use an immersive 3D platform that adheres to a building metaphor with underlying 3D models of offices, meeting halls, foyers, galleries, or libraries. In contrast, a virtual institute could also simply employ a text-based information system with communicative functions such as an enhanced email facility. Thus, virtual institutes can utilize different platforms to emphasize differing aspects of immersion and/or communication depending on the specific goals of the institute. For example, text-based chat systems allow virtual communities to flourish while single-user VRML scenes convey a highly immersive 3D environment that are only functional within certain contexts. Overall, there are three major emphasized areas of application: research, presentation, and communication. The Virtual Institute for Image Science (VIB) is described as a case study (3), and almost exclusively emphasizes communication as it allows individuals to perform joint projects despite being physically separated. Before covering the VIB in depth, we first provide a brief overview of virtual institutes between the poles of realistic immersion and of communication in a community (2), after which the VIB case study leads to general considerations regarding the balance virtual institutes must find between these bi-polar dimensions (4). Lastly, the concluding remarks focus on 3D technical tools currently available to virtual communities.

2   Between Immersion and Communication

The key issue spans the broad differences between the highly immersive VR applications, which allow for negligible communication between simultaneous users, and the essentially text-based focus of the initial virtual communities. Although the much-needed task of striking a balance between these two poles is not an easy one, existing virtual institutes and related research provides insight into a variety of potential solutions.

2.1 Pure 3D Presentation

On the far side of the scale, a real institute is represented by a 3D model of the building with little additional information to disturb the primary immersive function (e.g., Andrews 1993). These

Figure 1: Screenshot of a 3D model of the Computer Science Department building at Magdeburg (courtesy Kitty Stockfisch and Thomas Kientzler).

models are often constructed by computer science students (as seen in the new computer science building in Magdeburg in Figure 1) and typically used to inform new visitors, while the geometry data can be used in teaching and/or research as a demo or test data for new algorithms. Virtual institutes in this sense are quite similar to virtual museums and virtual architecture (cf. Buchholz & Schirra 2002).

2.2 3D Institutes with Synchronized HTML Pages

3D models of real buildings can also be combined with informative and relevant HTML presentations, as in the "Virtual Institute for Industrial Building Production" designed as a prototype (Kuhn 1999). This model forced Kuhn to resolve VR model issues concerning performance, authoring, and usability, wherein he ultimately synchronized two different HTML and VR windows automatically. The system depicts both 2D information and 3D desks (cf. Figure 2), with the latter containing buttons that start video conversations as the system does not allow users to actually meet in 3D space. Additionally, users can: set up "virtual desktops" to present objects related to current projects, use a meeting room containing a slide projector, and enter a room depicting a 3D graph of the relationships between institute members, projects and so on.

2.3 Virtual Institutes for Shared Interest Groups

Most web pages calling themselves "virtual institutes" are either homepages of academic institutes or homepages of special interest groups, with the former frequently founded as real institutional collaborations, such as *V.I.B.É: The Virtual Institute of Bioinformatics, Éire*, (http://www.bioinf.org). Both *The Virtual Institute of Mambila Studies*, about a people of Nigeria (http://lucy.ukc.ac.uk/VIMS) and our case study of *The Virtual Institute of Image Science* (VIB), are examples of the latter type of virtual institute.

2.4 Text-based Multi-User Dimensions (MUDs)

MediaMOO—an online media research community formed by Bruckman and Resnick (http://www.cc.gatech.edu/fac/Amy.Brucman/MediaMOO/), is a prototype of the text-based virtual institute, with the MUDs demanding imagination, and according to Marshall McLuhan, can be considered "hot media" (cf. Curtis 1996). Users navigate through command lines—with the disadvantage of needing to remember and write commands rather than using a GUI. Admittedly avatars, objects, and rooms can be easily created by typing a description,

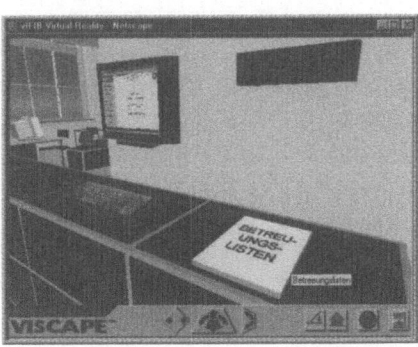

Figure 2: Snapshot from Kuhn's virtual institute
with a key element to a WWW page

and although harder than picking listed stock objects, this is notably easier than creating them via a 3D modeler.

Bruckman & Resnick liken their world to the spontaneous conversations that occur during conference breaks, emphasizing written talk as opposed to printable text (1993, cf. example below). A search engine (actually written by a user in the system's object-oriented programming language) allows participants to find chat partners with corresponding research interests.

An example from http://www.cc.gatech.edu/fac/Amy.Bruckman/MediaMOO/symposium-00.html:

Neon_Guest says, "'i'm wendy kellogg from ibm research. i manage a group called social computing."

[VWorlds] Hannes says, "My background is in computer science, but here at the medialab i'm working with professor Justine Cassel whose background is linguistics and psychology"

Neon_Guest says, "'we're working on building software to support distance collaboration for workgropus and have a particular slant on doing so that we call 'social translucence'"

[VWorlds] Amy says, "I guess we'll take advantage of the parallelism of the medium ;-)"

Neon_Guest says, "which really means trying to make PEOPLE andt their BEAHVIARIOVIOR more visiable"

Neon_Guest says, "i teyp good too ;-)"

[VWorlds] Hannes says, "We are essentially combining these fields to produce graphical embodiments of agents and online users that behave in a convincing fashion"

Neon_Guest says, "my background is in cognitive psychology and hci"

2.5 Communication Only (chat)

On the other side of the scale spanned in this section, a virtual institute consisting solely of chat channels exists without any spatial connotations via the IRC (Internet Relay Chat) standard or web-based software (like the *Virtual Institute Network*, http://polylab.sfu.ca/vin). Such a system is sufficient to set up and develop an "institute" with a pre-existing common interest group. Admittedly, an additional web page would effectively provide both an entry point into the chat system as well as an archive for transcripts and documents.

3   A Case Study: The Virtual Institute for Image Science (VIB)

The Virtual Institute of Image Science (VIB, cf. Fig. 3) was created to simplify the coordination of interdisciplinary projects within a community of art historians, computer scientists, communication scientists (including film theory and media theory), philosophers, psychologists, and social scientists concerned with aspects of image science. Currently, there are about 50 active VIB members and 100 passive members that comprise this very heterogeneous group with respect to computer-based media experience. Clearly, any electronic platform trying to ease the interactions and co-operations of such a group must take these preconditions into consideration.

The VIB was originally intended to support various interdisciplinary research projects and encourage ongoing future communication between geographically distant image scientists. Specifically, several book projects and conferences were organized, necessitating the coordination of all participants and authors, who were expected to discuss their views during the preparatory phases. Thus the VIB was installed as a preprint forum with restricted access (Sachs-Hombach & Schirra 2002). Although, the VIB software was finished as a rather unsatisfactory student project, our initial motivation in developing our own software, was to allow for controlled adaptations of the VIB and its changing needs. Additionally, issues characteristic of deadline-oriented projects arose wherein authors submitted "just in time", thus preempting the possibility of extended discussions or further coordination before publishing. Scientists (at least in the humanities) may also refuse viewing of individual papers in an unfinished

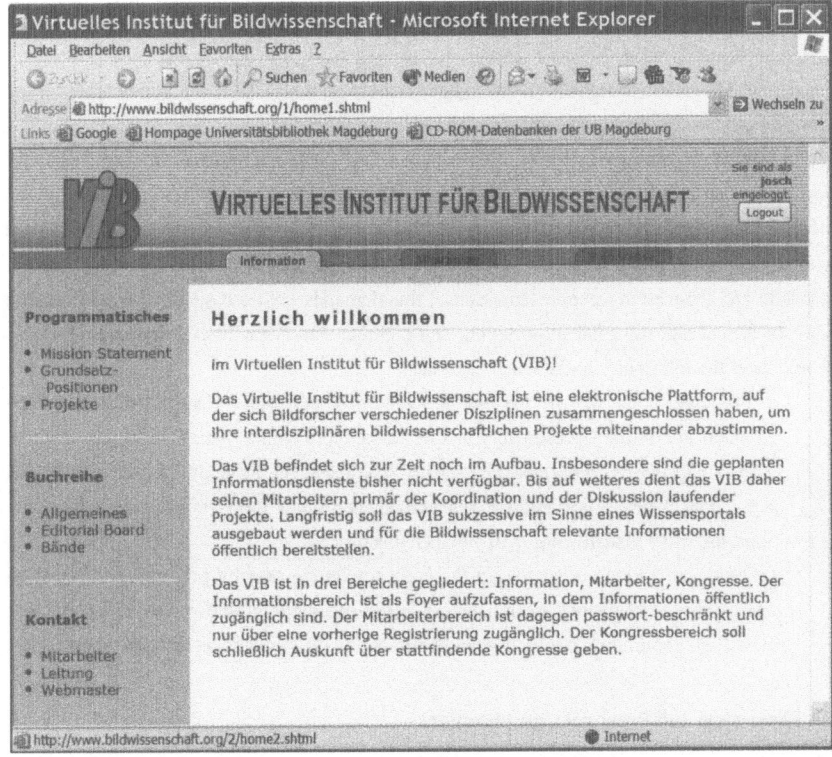

Figure 3: Entry page of the Virtual Institute for Image Science (VIB)

state. Ironically, this reserve disappears in face-to-face conversation during a conference where most scientists relish discussing their unfinished ideas, and points to the potential of 3D virtual meeting places as a tool for connecting authors within the VIB.

3.1 A Shift in Perspective for the VIB: Towards a Unified Image Science

Although the preprint forum did not work as intended, we developed many new and first-time connections between image scientists from different disciplines. This, in combination with a great deal of positive feedback and some funding allowed us to focus the VIB in a new direction: that of establishing a novel scientific approach to a "unified image science". The fundamental reason for the lack of such a science to date is largely attributed to its strongly interdisciplinary constitution, which—in the present scientific landscape of disciplinary separation, is inherently problematic. A science of images conceptually defines images as communicative entities or signs relying on both the special conditions of the communication media in question and the perceptual processes underlying image comprehension. Thus, unified image science investigates the nature and definition of "communication", "media", and "perception", and related issues (cf. Sachs-Hombach & Schirra 2002), which are traditionally explored separately, using different methodologies, and tend to focus on disparate portions of image use. Thus, the virtual institute of image science can now effectively compensate for the lack of a concrete institutional background.[1]

This shift in the conception of the VIB increases functional opportunities not only for members of the institute, but the general public as well. Although successfully implementing and maintaining an electronic platform demands certain specific intermediate goals, the initial goal is making the platform attractive to members, thus motivating further use for (a) accessing data, and (b) meeting people. In essence, this demands both a large database containing relevant formal and informal information, and communication facilities. Moreover, the VIB should meet the following fundamental criteria:

- *It stimulates informal discussions between members* while clearly indicating when members are online—presumably this would be more natural within 3D environments.
- *A variety of information (types) are easily visualized.* As the central motive of the VIB is to connect people of different scientific backgrounds from varied geographic locations, effective visualization will enhance this process.
- *Information is made attractive to the everyday image user* by presenting information interesting for laypeople. Establishing a larger surrounding platform as an entertaining 3D virtual community could ultimately attract other non-members into the central VIB.

3.2 Theoretical and Practical Considerations

The database demands adequate facilities to browse and search the site, as it essentially functions as library or media archive, wherein users can easily access texts and other relevant presentations such as talks, conferences, or research projects. Aside from user-friendliness, a "critical data mass" must be reached if the VIB is to remain sufficiently interesting, and could be achieved by encouraging all members to extend the data base accordingly. "If an individual is motivated in even a small way to benefit the group as a whole, the fact that digital public goods are purely non-rival can be a significant incentive to contribute toward the public good." (Kollock 1999, 225). Moreover, the heterogeneity of members and their contributions would better represent the range of relevant items to be incorporated into the database. Although, such divided labor necessitates an initial motivation, if all members contribute work personally deemed relevant, the data base will grow to such an extent as to remain interesting and potentially motivating further contributions.

Two aspects of the VIB database are of particular interest: First, images and their uses are fundamental to most of scientific research conducted within the VIB, thus demanding a multimedia database with pictures, films, and options to extended annotations. Indeed, as images

---

[1] Indeed, the VIB—as an application facilitating an unified image science, could provide revealing data on the nature of evolving interdisciplinary fields of research.

are increasingly important for presenting research results in an easily digestible and compact manner, the necessity for an effective multimedia database can be easily extended to other virtual institutes as well.

Secondly, the VIB as a 3D virtual environment is a paradigmatic application of image sciences, that is, a pictorial representation of image science. Although no new insights are actually achieved on this level for image science, the paradigmatic unity of the VIB, as a major representation of a science undergoing formalization, is a functional and aesthetic by-product that will be seen by potential members and others such as journalists (as representatives of the general public), members of funding boards, scientific organizations, and related industry.

The VIB is considering many key issues of privacy, which require many scientific institutions to maintain a limited access database for non-members, thus protecting internal affairs while giving the interested public an adequate impression of the institution's work. Public libraries, for example, for security purposes, use member cards, a rather complex secure file system for data administration, and a central database. The VIB also recognizes the importance of maintaining pre-defined restrictions for non-members, technical staff, ordinary members, and project chair persons as new ideas within scientific communities demand an "architecture of trust" (cf. Smith 2002). Thus, the VIB could offer secure individualized desktops for highly involved members and project groups, including fast or immediate access to that member's current database documents. Less involved members might not be provided with a secure individual desktop, but instead receive updates via a newsletter.

A central purpose for scientists spending time at the VIB is information access. Thus, this electronic community system may be largely viewed as a system "that encodes the knowledge of a community and provides an environment that supports the manipulation of that knowledge" (cf. Schatz 1993, 551). Even so, the underlying goal is to establish a novel scientific institution, which necessitates facilities to meet other interested members, effectively communicate, and eventually collaborate with them. Thus, the VIB must emphasize creation and maintenance of an easily accessible virtual environment as well as informational access, allowing for more than just member contact: to stimulate and support new projects, conference organization, other informal networking, while encouraging novel publication methodology such as reading, writing, rewriting, and reviewing texts together. As writing and publishing are scientifically sensitive, there must be further considerations of security, authentication, and access control. Thus, the VIB serves two main functions: (1) the dissemination of information among members, and (2) effective communication between members, with the emphasis on the latter function as it inherently supports information dissemination.

4   Discussion: The Balance between Immersion and Communication

The VIB can be functionally grouped according to immersion and communication needs, specifically distinguishing cooperative or group interactive tasks from those involving single users (cf. Table 1). Note that communication does not necessarily infer direct multi-user cooperation: for example, texts mediate communication without requiring all related participants to be present.

Table 1	Immersive task	Communicative task
Solitary task	Public showcase Orientation and leisure	Reading / Writing papers Searching the database
Cooperative task	Informal discussion Video conferencing ...	Formal meeting Passing documents ...

Image scientists, as all research scientists, must publish articles. In the particular context of a virtual institute, reading and writing texts are demanding solitary tasks demanding adequate screen space, a familiar user interface, high responsiveness, and a relatively undisturbed context. Consequently, a *complete* switch to a 3D environment for the VIB may have the disadvantage of forcing a majority of new users to initially struggle with usability issues as certain database functions, such as paper collections, are more user-friendly in classic web page form for solitary, non-immersive uses. Moreover, cooperative paper and research proposal depends on the solitary work of the co-authors to be coordinated with meetings and document exchange, such that web-based communication applications (file transfers, email, chat, and audio streaming) can be used in parallel with—or even replace, classical telecommunications such as telephone and fax.

However, "even with all those organizational and technical facilities at hand, it will still be very difficult to deal with the way of cooperation that researchers use most, namely the informal 'ad hoc encounter' that, via exchange of knowledge as well as gossip, opinions, etc., can lead to new research cooperation" (Lubich 1995, 73). Lubich lists a number of reasons for scientists to cooperate: specifically, solving specialized and interdisciplinary problems, building on other researchers' experience, receiving group funding, and cooperative teaching. Cooperation is typically associated with a specific, formal outcome: papers, journal, or research projects. "Although it is acknowledged that formal meetings, etc. are often part of a research cooperation, the emphasis is clearly on the informal part of cooperation, whose dynamics have been much less investigated and—in comparison to strictly formal interactions—are harder to model" (Lubich 1995, 67). Obviously, physical proximity plays a large role in successful scientific cooperation.

As these ad hoc encounters play such a key role within scientific communities, it is likely that certain 3D environments could support and even facilitate these interactions in mimicking the physical proximity between interlocutors. We recently created a 3D environment that accesses an online paper collection (cf. Figure 4) offered in the classical html page, which also functions as a virtual meeting place, such that the papers can be accessed simultaneously by several persons without using the 3D environment. When using the VR, simultaneous users are aware of each other as interested in the same paper of the collection, while a chat function allows them the space to informally discuss the papers or other issues.

Currently, the size and time of the online user population remains a major problem towards

Figure 4: Experimental 3D environment combining library and meeting place functions

• online papers can be accessed in a separate browser window by clicking the posters showing bibliographic data and abstracts;

• users, appearing as avatars, can directly chat with each other (e.g., about the papers)

the functionality of such a 3D meeting place is. Specifically, the chance to really meet somebody else (anybody!) without having an explicit appointment is usually quite small if the site is not visited by thousands of users a day. Here, we return to the issue of motivating enough users to achieve that initial critical mass for functionality before there exists a good probability of actually meeting someone of interest. If the VR can attract enough users, it then becomes a *working* meeting place: provided that a relatively closed group of users with common interests and other paths of communication would perceive the effort necessary to entering the virtual meeting place as worthwhile. Otherwise the members will likely not return and resort to what they know works: telephone and email.

Informal meetings in a real institute can be compared to the typical coffee break or "water cooler encounters" when members "run into each other" at the coffee machine or water cooler, leading to spontaneous conversation about any number of topics, which in turn, may lead to a new collaboration or concept. Similarly, the breaks offered at conferences and workshops provide the time and space for an informal conversation that might catalyze further scientific collaboration.

Obviously, the VIB would induce few of these spontaneous encounters with a virtual coffee machine as it does not fulfill the criterion which allows for a real coffee break encounter: (1)

Table 2	immersive task	communicative task
solitary task	*functionality of virtual realities*	*classical single-user interfaces*
cooperative task	*VR with multi-user communication and other coordination functions*	*functionality of virtual communities (without disguise)*

the physiological need for the members to move physically to that place with (2) no immediate intention to work while (3) also being open for social interaction. The second and third criterion are both maintained within a VR and are important because the intention to work would certainly reduce socializing opportunities. Thus, a plausible adjustment to the virtual institute must be found for the first point, wherein physiological motivation for a coffee break, must be replaced by some motivating factor which allows for members to pass unobtrusively through the virtual meeting room. If database access were channeled exclusively through a virtual meeting room, it would be reminiscent of the foyer of a library—essentially offering a place for unplanned encounters that take place while waiting for books or studying conference posters or ads on the wall. Criterion (2) partially fulfilled as work that one intends to do occurs in other rooms (in silence) may be postponed for a quick chat in the foyer.

The range of non-verbal signals occurring during these informal "real" interactions is a fundamental and highly relevant consideration in informal computer-mediated communication in a 3D environment: from facial expression to vocal intonation, body language to eye contact, many expressive background signs enrich the verbal foreground and have an enormous impact on the overall content of communication. Presumably, the absence of these signals would make many scientists hesitate to share unfinished scripts with colleagues, although they would unflinchingly discuss the same draft face to face (Smith 2002, 59). We must continue to consider the merits of integrating *viva voce* communication and video conferencing, as it remains doubtful whether relatively rigid avatars and written chat are truly immersive enough for the intended virtual meeting. Whether a 3D environment can effectively imitate these informal encounters so necessary to scientific cooperation remains mainly an empirical question, depending heavily on the quality of the 3D environment, as well as the more practical, but necessary cost-benefits analysis.

The VIB immersive and communicative tasks defined within Table 1 are incorporated into Table 2 according to task functionality—specifically in terms of the previous discussion. While solitary communicative tasks are most effective without overloading the interfaces in too much "virtuality", solitary immersive tasks and cooperative communicative tasks calls for a specific form of virtuality provided by pure VR's or the broader virtual communities respectively. Admittedly, solitary immersion remains more of an aesthetic display useful for public relations, while communicative cooperation is highly relevant to the VIB, and—apart from character disguise, all the features available to virtual communities are applicable. Only cooperative immersive tasks encompass the qualities of an informal meeting, demand the full combination of VR with the synchronized interaction of virtual communities. As seen in the "coffee break" metaphor, setting details and considerations are critical: specifically, how to create and maintain a natural motivation within members and nonmembers to drive daily use of the VIB. Support potential lies in the natural integration of other functions.

5   Conclusions: Technical Requirements

Each sub task collected for the VIB determines an optimal point of balance between immersion and communication, wherein all tasks must be adequately integrated, merging on a common technical basis that provides the necessary freedom to effectively meet the varied demands. The VIB is implemented into the well established WWW application to ease interface, programming, and maintenance needs, while allowing users to read, download, and upload documents, as well as clearly supporting information dissemination. Moreover, the WWW supports synchronous communication functions like chat and can be extended to support additional media types such as 3D scenes.

Historically, the WWW has been successful because browsers could support previous protocols (i.e. the *file transfer protocol* (ftp) and *gopher* (Berners-Lee 1996) as well as allowing for easy authoring and information distribution. We expect that collaboration and synchronous communication facilities – starting with text chat, including (but not limited to) voice and video communication – will need to be packaged into a single, user-friendly application available on many platforms and extendable at run-time in order to be ready for wide-spread use.

The web-based 3D tool 'Atmosphere' developed by Adobe is available in its beta version for Windows and Mac operating systems and offers many of the options necessary to a more immersive virtual institute. Indeed, the virtual library depicted in Figure 4 was developed on this platform, as well as numerous other examples of now-established VRs and virtual communities. Currently, the platform's distribution is free, with an automatic installation of the browser plug-in necessary to enter an "atmosphere world" upon opening the corresponding web page. Access to external web pages may be integrated by means of JavaScript, or other applications such as database access. Currently redirected chat channels are utilizing an intermediate web-based machine translator, while a direct integration of voice communication, in conjunction with standard chat, is now experimentally established.

With an extension to the 3D environment 'Croquet' currently under way (www.opencroquet.org, Fig. 5), 'Squeak' (Guzdial and Rose 2002, cf. www.squeak.org) is a

Figure 5: A screenshot from Croquet: The "picture objects" are portals

multimedia platform promising to provide suitable technical support for the VIB.[2] Moreover, Croquet is freely available, runs on a number of platforms, and contains sophisticated synchronization mechanisms. Although it requires a central server computer for login notification, it does not need one for communication between browsers, and supports the user-based creation and programming of objects through Smalltalk (an object-oriented programming language with a long history).[3]

Finally, how should participation in the development of the VIB's technical infrastructure be delegated to the members? Although, the VIB cannot be an inadaptable monolithic block for all users, architectural alterations must be carefully defined in terms of the user. If members are enabled to greatly alter the VIB, those not familiar with the multimedia tools necessary for orchestrating such change may find such potential overwhelming and even stressful. The informal cooperation expressed by chatting with other members and the technical staff would be more helpful in improving self-organization of the institute's technical infrastructure than expecting members to directly re-program system components. On the other hand, providing basic building blocks to the infrastructure that can be created and arranged in a user-friendly interface could prove valuable in particular for designing project-specific ar-

---

[2] Working on both Squeak's development team and at the Department of Simulation and Graphics, A. Raab, could easily create customized features for the VIB.

[3] Indeed, Croquet utilizes Smalltalk, and if desired, graphics can be programmed at a similarly low level.

eas—including, for example, restricted access to project documents and the meeting room—without the help of the technical staff.

Installing a virtual institute that supports the formalization of a new interdisciplinary scientific approach demands a broad variety of functions offered to both members and the public. These functions can be classified according to the kind of virtuality in which they are best employed: between immersion and communication, solitary and cooperative tasks contribute to aspects of VRs and virtual communities to various degrees. As a special kind of virtual communities, virtual institutes are paradigmatic cases for combining immersive and communicative functionalities, and provide an interesting research domain regarding the relevant functionality of novel 3D platforms. However, the user's motivation to enter a highly immersive virtual institute must be initially enhanced and eventually maintained by carefully integrating and adapting tasks to the specific needs of the corresponding shared interest group.

References

Andrews, K. (1993): Constructing Cyberspace: VR and Hypermedia. In: VR Vienna '93: ftp://ftp.iicm.edu/pub/papers/vrv93.ps.gz (as of April 2003).

Berners-Lee, T. (1996): The World Wide Web: Past, Present and Future. Online paper: http://www.w3.org/People/Berners-Lee/1996/ppf.html (as of April 2003).

Bruckman, A., Resnick, M. (1993): Virtual Professional Community: Results from the MediaMOO project. In: Proceedings of 3CyberConf, The Third International Conference on Cyberspace: http://citeseer.nj.nec.com/bruckman93virtual.html (as of April 2003).

Buchholz, K., Schirra, J.R.J. (2002): Das Haus als Gesamtkunstwerk: eine Herausforderung an die Computervisualistik. In: Sachs-Hombach, K. (ed.): Bildhandeln. Magdeburg: Scriptum, pp. 241-268.

Curtis, P. (1996): Mudding: Social Phenomena in Text-Based Virtual Realities. In: Stefik, M. (ed.): Internet Dreams: Archetypes, Myths, and Metaphors. Cambridge: MIT Press, pp. 265-292.

Guzdial, M., Rose, K. (2002): Squeak: Open Personal Computing and Multimedia. Upper Saddle River: Prentice Hall.

Heim, M. (1998): Virtual Realism, Oxford: OUP.

Kollock, P. (1999). The Economies of Online Cooperation: Gifts and Public Goods in Cyberspace. In: Kollock, P. & Smith, M. (eds.): Communities in Cyberspace. New York: Routledge, pp. 220-239.

Kuhn, R. (1999): Virtuelles Institut – ein multimediales Informationssystem als interaktive Internet-Schnittstelle zwischen Benutzer und Hochschul-Institut. Master's Thesis, Institute for Industrial Building Production, University of Karlsruhe: http://www.ubka.uni-karlsruhe.de/cgi-bin/psview?document=1998/architektur/1 (as of April 2003)

Lubich, H.P. (1995): Towards a CSCW Framework for Scientific Cooperation in Europe. Lecture Notes in Computer Science 889. Berlin, Heidelberg, New York: Springer-Verlag.

Mynatt, E.D., Adler, A., Ito, M., O'Day, V.L. (1997): Design for Network Communities. Proc. of the ACM Conf on Human Factors in Computing Systems (CHI '97), Atlanta, USA, 1997, pp. 210-217.

Sachs-Hombach, K., Schirra, J.R.J. (2002): Von der interdisziplinären Grundlagenforschung zur computervisualistischen Anwendung: Die Magdeburger Bemühungen um eine allgemeine Wissenschaft vom Bild. Magdeburger Wissenschaftsjournal 1/2002, Magdeburg, pp. 27-38.

Schatz, B.R. (1993): Building an Electronic Community System. In: Ronald M. Baecker (ed.). Readings in Groupware and Computer-Supported Cooperative Work. San Francisco: Morgan Kaufmann, pp. 550-560.

Smith, J.H., (2002): The Architectures of Trust – Supporting Cooperation in the Computer-Supported Community. Master's Thesis, Department of Film and Media Studies, University of Copenhagen: http://www.gamasutra.com/education/theses/20020410/smith.pdf (as of April 2003).

Computational Visualistics at the Otto-von-Guericke University of Magdeburg

THOMAS STROTHOTTE

This paper gives an informal introduction to computational visualistics, tracing its roots, surveying its current focus and suggesting directions for the future of the area.

Background

In the early 1990s, all academic programs at the University of Magdeburg, being located in the former East Germany, were restructured and redesigned as a consequence of the Berlin Wall falling in November, 1989. It was a time when very few local East German high-school graduates took up their university studies at their home-town universities, preferring universities in what was known up to that point as West Germany. The lure of the "golden west" meant that universities like the one in Magdeburg were forced to re-evaluate their mission if they were to survive.

By the same token, the early 90s were an exciting time for academic staff at the University of Magdeburg. Many new professors were hired within a period of a few years, all eager to forge new ties to other disciplines. New faculty members generally had considerable time on their hands to meet among one another and lead academic discussions.

It was in this atmosphere that a group of faculty members began meeting in October, 1994 to talk about "pictures". They came from the Faculties of Computer Science, Mechanical Engineering, Electrical Engineering, Medicine, as well as Arts and Education. The group soon discovered that they had common interests, despite the fact that the methods and tools of their disciplines differed immensely. A lecture series was formed, and ideas were generated how the common ground could be exploited. Besides common ground in research questions was the realization that a new discipline was emerging which would have long-term significance. After about 18 months of research and planning, an undergraduate degree programme in computational visualistics was born.

Computational Visualistics as an Academic Discipline

Computational Visualistics is defined as the area of academic endeavour which studies the generation and analysis of images by computers and humans. The term was chosen to emphasise the analogy to language: What computational linguistics does for language, computational visualistics does for images. The focal point of this discipline lies within computer science, since this area provides the most important methods and tools for today's treatment of pictures.

At the time the term Computational Visualistics was coined, quite a number of alternative terms were considered. Among these were "Bildwissenschaft" ("Image Science", or "Imaging Science"), "Bildinformatik" ("Image Computing"), but also "Medieninformatik ("Media Informatics"). Although in some cases the latter term now includes what we refer to as computational Visualistics, media informatics is also used for other topics, particularly referring to audio and video technology. The terms "Imaging Science" and "Image Science" have been used in the literature particularly for the study of processes of producing images from numerical data, and were considered too narrow for what was to be expressed. By contrast, the term finally chosen, computational visualistics expresses well what is referred to in the definition: dealing with visualizations by computer.

Perhaps the most fundamental realization underlying this new discipline is that pictures have become more than just a representation of information. Instead, in many disciplines like medicine, two dimensional data which can be mapped onto a colour scale is the actual output of physical processes, and a mapping of such data onto pixels of a computer screen is often straight forward. Hence a sonograph has as its output images which are analysed by an examining physician; algorithms accessible to doctors generally do not try to analyse the underlying data; if anything, algorithms are designed to post-process the image produced by the sonograph. This shift to treating two dimensional as the raw data and analysing or interacting with it, rather than producing a stream of data and either analysing it statistically or producing images as an end-product is what the author interprets as the iconic turn often referred to in the literature (see for example Bredenkamp, 1997).

Studying Computational Visualistics

Undergraduate Program

At the University of Magdeburg a five-year undergraduate degree program leading to a "Diplomingenieur für Computervisualistics" (MSc in Computational Visualistics) was established in 1996 (see Strothotte and Schirra, 1998, and Schirra, 2000). From its inception it consistently attracted about 50% more students than the degree program in computer science, and this trend continues to the present year (Fall 2003). After the start-up phase, the program has averaged about 150 new students per year. About one-third of these are women (compared to under 10% women in computer science programs) and also about one-third are out-of-state students, which is also significantly higher than other degree programs at the university.

The degree program encompasses just over 50% computer science courses. This percentage is significant in several ways. First, it expresses the underlying sentiment that a modern-day preoccupation with images is computer-centered. Second, it gives graduates a sound basis in computer science so that when they turn to looking for employment after graduation, they are equipped to work everywhere where normally a computer scientist would work – yet are better qualified for such jobs that deal with images and user interfaces. Finally, this makes it possible for the degree program to be accredited as a computer science degree.[1] The 50% computer science content in computational visualistics compares to about 65% computer science content in comparable computer science degrees.

The remaining 50% of the degree program are divided into about 15% for the mathematics and physics education needed to understand processes underlying computing, 20% in the arts, education and humanities, and 15% in an application subject.

The courses in the arts, education and humanities cover topics such as psychological processes for understanding images, studies in education on learning with images, political issues with respect to the use of images to influence public opinion, philosophical questions pertaining to what pictures really are, and the design of user interfaces. Here the students generally attend lectures which are also offered to students of the respective fields of study. An important effect of the courses is that while students are studying their primary field of interest, images, they are exposed to and need to develop skills in the arts and humanities. We expect the graduates to develop into more well-rounded personalities than students who study exclusively a technical subject.

Finally, the courses in an application subject are intended to give students an in-depth insight into the use of images. As freshmen, students choose one of the following five application subjects:

- Medicine,
- Material Science (offered by the Faculty of Mechanical Engineering),
- Computer-Aided Design and Manufacturing (Mechanical Engineering),
- Image Information Science (Electrical Engineering), and
- Audiovisual Media (Education).

Through these courses, students are taught to speak to and understand scientists of a different discipline, to understand their imaging needs, and to solve their problems using methods and tools from computer science based on an understanding of their users' needs as perceived on the basis of their background in the arts, humanities and education. While it is not the expectation that graduates will necessarily work in the application area they studied, this part of their education is to equip them with the necessary understanding to approach any application area and to solve the problems which arise. Indeed, this is the normal situation which computational visualists will encounter in the later careers: To solve others' imaging problems by first understanding what the problem really is, and then applying their own methods and tools.

Students carry out a six month industrial internship during the first half of their 4th year of studies. This enables future employers to test students before they graduate and gives the

---

[1] The "accreditation" referred to here is to be considered a degree program in computer science by the German Council of Computer Science Deans ("Fakultätentag Informatik").

University the possibility to carry out marketing activities for the new degree program. Many students are placed with companies active in their application subject, while others go into different application areas.

Finally, a "Diplomarbeit" (thesis) is written in the last six months of the degree program.

Graduate Program

An internationally-oriented master's program in computational Visualistics was established at the University of Magdeburg in 1997. About 10 to 15 students are enrolled every year. With all courses offered in English, the program is of interest to international students who come from all over the world.

Finally, it is possible to complete a PhD degree in computational Visualistics. The first PhD graduate in this area (Stefan Schlechtweg) completed his degree in September, 1999. The University of Koblenz-Landau also offers a PhDs program in computational Visualistics and granted their first such degree a few months later.

Perspectives

While computational visualistics as an area of study is now firmly established – a similar program was started at the University of Koblenz-Landau in 1998 – transdisciplinary studies are now beginning to emerge. Indeed, a number of papers in the present volume describe results of such research as is carried out at the University of Magdeburg.[2]

One area which the author considers ripe for investigation on a broad scale is the role of images in virtual communities. Thanks to the immense processing power of new PC-based graphics hardware, it will become possible to devise a new generation of browsers whose navigation is based on images rather than the text-based navigation of current Netscape or Internet Explorer functionality. This will enable users with like interests to more easily take up contact with one another. An important area of application is learner communities in which students studying a subject can team up systematically or in an ad hoc manner to form study or discussion groups. We expect this to be a long-term topic of transdiscplinary scientific interest.

References

Bredenkamp, Horst, "Metaphors of the End in the Era of Images", in H. Klotz (Ed.), Contemporary Art, Prestel, Munich – New York, 1997, pp. 32–37.

Strothotte, Thomas and Jörg R.J. Schirra, "Computervisualistik: Ein Diskussionsbeitrag zur universitären Ausbildung im Bereich Multimedia", in J. Dassow and R. Kruse (Eds.), *Informatik zwischen Bild und Sprache. Informatik '98 – Proceedings der GI-Jahrestagung*

---

[2] See in particular the contributions by Halper et al., Marotzki et al., Sachs-Hombach et al. and Tönnies et al.

1998, pp. 365–376, Berlin – Heidelberg – New York, 1998. Gesellschaft für Informatik, Springer-Verlag.

Schirra, Jörg R.J., "A New Theme for Educating New Engineers: Computational Visualistics", *Global Journal of Engineering Education*, 4(1), pp. 73-82, June 2000.

Web Sites

www.computervisualistik.de

Degree program in computational Visualistics at the University of Magdeburg

http://www.uni-koblenz.de/~lb/visualistik/vis/vis.html

Degree program in computational Visualistics at the University of Koblenz-Landau

Virtual Communities:
Trust, Identity, Participation, and Technology

WINFRIED MAROTZKI, JANA DITTMANN, FRANK LESSKE

Motivation of the Triangle of Trust, Identity and Technology

The complexity of societies, which grows in proportion to the application of new technologies, inevitably also has an effect on the lives of individuals. In this context, one key component of social interactions comes into focus: trust. Since the 1990's, we have seen an increasing number of publications regarding the topic of trust written from a range of perspectives including those of sociology, education, philosophy, political science, and economics. Here, trust is assumed to be a basic precondition of all social processes, but when trust is not longer self-evident the relative importance of re-building trust increases in turn. In other words, trust, as a phenomenon, comes into the focus of systematic reflection.

In our paper we discuss those social environments in which trust building becomes necessary as they tend to be directly related to available new information technologies. In the following we first overview trust as a phenomenon in the social sciences, and secondly, observe trust in the computer sciences, and in terms of computer security, after which, we provide a brief summary. In chapter two a visualization model is introduced that describes varying degrees of trustworthiness as functions of trust, identity and technology. Finally, we consider integration and implementation of this model in terms of virtual communities, and conclude with a summary of future work.

Social Sciences View

To summarise the social scientists' view on trust: it is an essential component of social interaction as it (1) reduces complexity in the physical dimension, (2) creates stable frameworks for active and interactive processes in the social dimension, and (3) can serve to bridge ignorance within the temporal dimension (cf. in detail: Endress 2002, pp. 10-27). Trust is a basic social mechanism recognizing the fundamental that no action is truly risk-free as actions tend to occur with insufficient knowledge. Because individual autonomy is virtually nonexistent, the necessity of trust becomes apparent as it serves to bridge informational and temporal uncertainties between individuals.

Luhmann (cf. 1968) differentiates between *personal trust*—in individuals, and *systemic trust*—in social and technical systems. While controlling systemic trust demands learned, professional knowledge of such things as technical systems, controlling personal trust obviously does not. Additionally, there is an observable shift from the dominance of [inter]personal trust within small, relatively undifferentiated societies towards a type of systemic trust typical to complex, highly differentiated and technically orientated societies.

Similarly, Anthony Giddens (1996) argues that modernization is characterized by individuals becoming more fixed within their concrete, temporally, and locally bound interaction contexts, while demanding a rise in personal reflexivity, wherein people must be singly accountable for an increasing number of decisions. Thus, the more technology moves to support information, communication, and all social interactions between human beings and their natural environment, the more humans must rely on systemic trust.

Giddens (cf. 1996, p. 49) defines the concept of trust as confidence in the reliability of a person or of a system concerning a given amount of results or events. Thus, trust is a state of mind reflecting a level of faith in the perceived reliability of a person, institution, or technology. Giddens focuses specifically on the institutional mediation of systemic trust, wherein the nature of modern institutions is greatly related to the mechanisms of trust in abstract systems—especially in expert systems (e.g., the relation between physician and patient), which are typical examples of institutional frameworks and institutionalised patterns of trust (e.g., insurance systems). In a way, one may think of these and foundations testing consumer goods ("Stiftung Warentest") or consumer rights organisations, as 'intermediary institutions of trust.'

The relation of rationality and trust as elaborated by James S. Coleman (1991), identifies the following structural patterns as characteristic of the logic of trust:

(1) To trust implies the transference of resources.

(2) If the trusted person is trustworthy, the 'trustee' accordingly improves their position, or otherwise accordingly worsens their position.

(3) The transference of resources occurs without the recipient taking on any real obligation.

(4) To assess the appropriateness of trust implies a temporal delay until the time when trust pays off (cf. Endress 2002, p. 36).

Thus, according to Coleman, the decision to trust is directly related to the trusting person's knowledge or evaluation of potential losses and achievable surplus. The relevance of this knowledge demonstrates the importance of providing information or proof that the trust relationship is worthwhile, if only because individuals—as rational actors give trust in a rational way when the expected advantage (proof of achievable surplus) is higher than the expectable possible disadvantage (potential loss). This implies a model of one-sided allocation of trust, wherein the phenomenal area of trust is rather reduced (Endress 2002), as the gaining and distribution of information is merely a strategic action pattern to assess trustworthiness.

The problem of Identity

Identity can be conceived of in terms of its formal, personal, and role definitions. *Formal identity* confers to the identification of the respective offline-person, in that it is guaranteed that behind each online-person (e.g. an avatar) there is a specific offline-person and would identify the online-user on an offline-basis. This is not only important for Internet auction facilities such as eBay, but also for online communities. Offline-persons who act and build up social relationships online must ensure that the online-persons they initially encounter are actually the same person upon subsequent encounters. The importance attached to this type of formal identity varies according to different communities, as denoted by the fact that nicknames are traditionally not acceptable. But even though many game communities typically employ nicknames or arbitrarily constructed avatars, it is still important in the development of a culture of trust to know that a single real person is definitely behind one and the same online-person.

The *personal identity* confers the identity of a real person as given in an online environment. As a rule this concerns a list of self-chosen characteristics, which can be seen via the identity card but may also be changed by the person. *Role identity* or social identity unfolds in the social actions of the virtual space, wherein specific roles develop—such as the individual knowing more of the technical aspects of formula-one racing, thus creating role-specific reputations or identities. In combination with formal and personal identity, we conceive *trust* as the aforementioned cluster of characteristics, while *technology* comprises all forms of hard- and software implementations (cf. Winkel 1999).

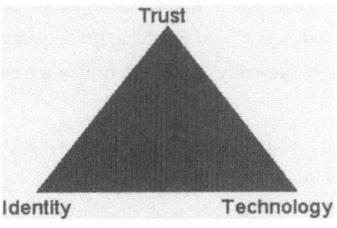

– Figure 1 –

The triangle of trust, identity, and technology is defined as follows: (1) a *culture of trust* is necessary both for the development and maintenance of the three-fold identity and acceptance of the technological design or systemic trust; (2) personal and role *identity* is necessary both to developing a culture of trust and the creative provision of respective technology facilities; and lastly, (3) technological designs are necessary for both developing and sustaining identity, and a culture of trust. The following further elaborates the components of this triangle.

The View of Technology

Trust is a belief—in the field of computer technology regarding hard- and software implementations, that a computer entity will do what it should to protect resources and be safe from attack, see Bishop (2003), page 477. In a more precise definition of computer security, trust is described in terms of trustworthiness, wherein "[a]n entity is trustworthy if there is sufficient credible evidence leading one to believe that the system will meet a set of given requirements. Trust is a measure of trustworthiness, relying on the evidence provided" (page 478). To properly capture the degrees of trust means to measure confidence in whether and to what degree an entity fits its informed requirements. To properly quantify trust, the term 'security assurance' specifies the degree to which one can trust a system, (page 487) such that assurance is classified as a "confidence that an entity meets its requirements, based on specific evidence provided by the application of assurance techniques".

In the following we summarize main security requirements and enumerate common security measures taken to ensure the execution of these requirements, see also Dittmann et al. (2001):

Confidentiality: Cipher systems or steganography are used to keep information secret from unauthorized entities, such that confidentiality also concerns aspects of secrecy or privacy.

Data integrity: The alteration of data can be detected by means of one-way hash functions, message authentication codes, digital signatures (especially content-based digital signatures), fragile digital watermarking. Beside data integrity the term integrity can be summarized as preventing corruption, impairment, or modification of information, services, or equipment.

Data origin authenticity: Message authentication codes, digital signatures, fragile digital watermarking, and robust digital watermarking to enable proof of origin.

Entity authenticity: Entities taking part in a communication can be proven by authentication protocols, which ensure an entity is who it claims to be. In general, authenticity is proof that a person or other agent has been correctly identified, or that a message is stored and received as transmitted.

Non-repudiation: proof of whether a particular event or action occurred such as the generation, sending, receipt, submission, or transport of a message. Non-repudiation certificates, tokens, and protocols establish information accountability based on message authentication codes or digital signatures combined with notary services, time-stamping services and evidence recording.

Availability: proof that information, services, and equipment are working and available for use, such as firewall techniques for filtering in-and outgoing data, data replication, large-scaled and redundant networks and computing power (Northcutt et al. 2003).

The security measures mentioned above use cryptographic or steganographic mechanisms and digital watermarking as technical security measures. A short introduction to approaches is given in Dittmann et al. (2000) for multimedia systems while Bishop (2003) or Stallings (2003) cover a wide variety of further measures such as:

- Physical security measures (e.g., physical locks)
- Organizational security measures (e.g., regulations concerning employees behaviour determination of access rights to sensitive data)
- Audit measures (e.g., guidelines for actions to be taken when security requirements are violated)
- User training and education programs designed to reduce security exposures as well as define security policies for legal purposes;
- Institutional measures (e.g., standardization, certification based on soft- and hardware requirements or Computer Emergency Response Teams (like CERT))
- More security requirements can be found at http://www.semper.org/sirene-/outsideworld/standard.html.

Within IT security, explicit security policy expectations can be summarized in the differing security levels—from low to high, which handles any remaining risk, while assurances provide the justification that the given measures actually meet policy demands via evidence and subsequent policy approval. The implemented mechanisms are entities that are created and applied to meet the requirements of that policy. A trusted system can be defined as a "system that has been shown to meet well-defined requirements under an evaluation by a credible body of experts who are certified to assign trust ratings to evaluated products and systems" (Bishop, page 479).

Within virtual communities, trust incorporates both aspects of the social sciences in terms of application design and systemic trust in terms of hard- and software design and applications. As previously mentioned, the correct identity determination is an essential precondition to build trust in an online environment, as identity theft and the use of multiple identities are both common occurrences in this setting. Indeed, identity theft incidents are continuously reported (see for example

http://www.chicagotribune.com/technology/columnists/chi-030204techcrime,0,5153517.story (2003)). Thus, the eBay trust model must consider that the more identity theft and loss of reputation occurs, the more individual user profiles become questionable, thereby weakening if not ultimately destroying trust within online business interactions as well as the entire online social system. Technically speaking, there are three possible methods of authentication: (1) *possession* (what you have); (2) *knowledge* (what you know); and, (3) *biometrics* (beings, like unique personal traits) see more details for example in Bishop (2003). Clearly, the quality of the achieved security level dictates the overall systemic trust as well as personal trust between users. A further consideration is the fact that the development of identity also implies the potential for developing techniques to support pseudo-anonymity, anonymity, group identity, (cf. Chaum 1985, Köhntopp & Pfitzmann 2000).

Visualization: Clarity Builds Trust

Because the attributes of trust as defined within social interactions, technology, and identity are essential to the support and construction of trustworthy systems such as virtual communities, we are able to clearly visualize our three measures via the triangle construct:

- Trust as Condition of Identity and Technology
- Technology as Condition of Trust and Identity
- Identity as Condition of Trust and Technology

The construction of a visual metaphor clarifies the role of trust in determining individual user trust levels within a virtual community according to their position within the community.

- *Minimized isosceles triangle*: a minimum trust guarantee for all three determinants, for example the user enters a region where trust levels on all accounts decrease.

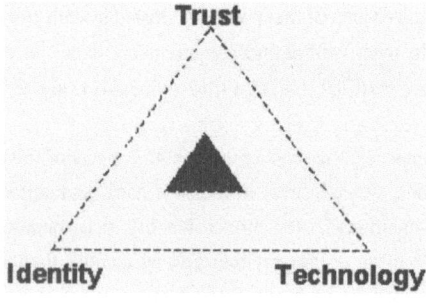

– Figure 2 –

- Maximized, non-isosceles triangle: a maximum trust guarantee for identity-based trust while levels are significantly lower for technology. For example, several known attacks to the system are accepted and any remaining risk can be effectively handled.

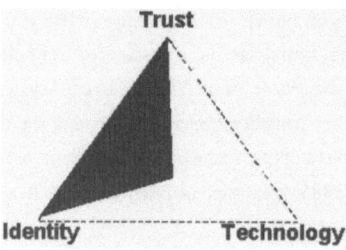

– Figure 3 –

- Edge trust and technology: no successful identity verification took place.

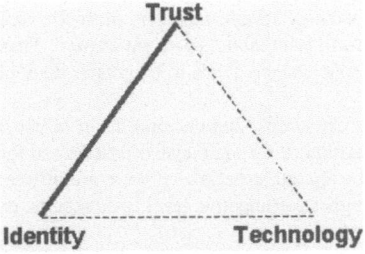

– Figure 4 –

- Salient angle trust: the trust depends solely on socially determined trust, with no technical mechanisms available for supporting trust or determining identity.

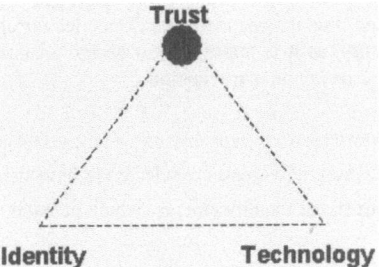

– Figure 5 –

To visualize the quality of mechanisms employed, we introduce circles as salient angles of the triangle, wherein these angles and the respective diameters indicate the expected trust level, while colours of different degrees or transitions can indicate differences between trust levels.

Integration of Participation

From a social and political science point of view, these triangles hold interesting implications for how trust in others depends heavily on the quality and importance of a given interaction. Moreover, any social system can be differentiated according to interdependent but separately considered components: (1) the *building* of social environments by establishing systemic social rules for 'high-quality-interaction'; and (2) the *changing and modulating* of these social systems, as interactions with a gradually lower scale of interaction-quality. Thus, a clear connection emerges between the trust identity and technology triangle and the *participation* occurring therein.

- When building a social system, participation and systemic trust are clearly linked, in that the more we participate in creating and establishment a system, the greater our systemic trust tends to be.

- When an participating in changing an existing social system, individuals need both systemic trust and personal trust as social rules and systems can not be changed by one single person, but by social groups. If a social system individual lead (in computers, an administrator; in politics, a dictator), several members must first react by disobeying, ignoring, abusing, or avoiding it, to bring about systemic change. Thus, trust—in terms of participating in driving systemic change, tends to be greater than what is necessary for initially building a system.
- Participation is highly demanding and essential form of cooperation between individuals in a social system, thus requiring a high level of stability in formal identity, otherwise participative rights may be abused, especially if there are differentiated levels of such as administrators holding higher participative level than experts, experts higher than users, users higher than guests.
- Although participation and participative rights can be regulated, and hierarchically structured via groups or levels according to available technology, technology can be also regulated by participation and is extremely important for the implementation of security infrastructures. As long as many or all individuals can participate in the security decisions of a given (social) system, the danger of abusing certain groups' rights is low, but if participative rights are reduced, this danger increases. Thus, technical security and participation tend to be contradictory, as it is impossible to design an infrastructure combining both maximum security and maximum participation.

Moreover, once participatory issues of *representation*—for groups of exceeding a certain size, are considered—in that certain individuals are selected to have more rights to participate than others, further issues of trust and identity emerge, which demand new technological arrangements.

Summary and Further Work

In summary, there are a wide variety of factors influencing trust within virtual communities, such that future challenges are threefold: (1) determination of the concrete requirements, attributes, levels and mechanisms for trust, technology and identity for virtual communities; (2) a precise design of the triangle in size, colour, states, and transitions; and (3) comprehensive integration of participation and representation issues for visualization within the triangle as a pyramid.

References

Bishop, M. 2003. *Computer Security - Art and Science*. Boston (Addison-Wesley).

Chaum, D. 1985. "Security without Identification: Transaction Systems to Make Big Brother Obsolete". *Communications of the ACM 28*, 10, P. 1030-1044. (Updates version: http://www.chaum.com/articles/Security_Wthout_Identification.htm.)

Coleman, J. S. 1991. *Grundlagen der Sozialtheorie. Bd. 1: Handlungen und Handlungssysteme*. München (Oldenbourg).

Dittmann, J.; Wohlmacher, P.; Nahrstedt, K. 2001. "Multimedia and Security – Using Cryptographic and Watermarking Algorithms", *IEEE MultiMedia*, October-December 2001, Vol. 8, No. 4, pp. 54-65, ISSN 1070-986X.

Endress, M. 2002. *Vertrauen*. Bielefeld (Transcript).

Giddens, A. 1996. *Konsequenzen der Moderne*. Frankfurt a.M. (Suhrkamp).

Köhntopp, M., A. Pfitzmann. 2000. "Datenschutz Next Generation". In: Bäumler, Hg. E-Privacy. *Proc. Sommerakademie des Unabhängigen Landeszentrums für Datenschutz Schleswig-Holstein*, 28. August 2000 in Kiel. Wiesbaden: Vieweg, S. 316-322.

Luhmann, N. 1968. *Vertrauen. Ein Mechanismus der Reduktion sozialer Komplexität*. 4. Auflage 2000. Stuttgart (Lucius & Lucius).

Northcutt, S.; Zeltser, L.; Winters, S.; Frederick K.K.; Ritchey, R.W. (2003): *Inside Network Perimeter Security*. Indiana (New Riders (Pearson Education)).

Rössler, P.; Wirth, W. (Hrsg.) (1999): *Glaubwürdigkeit im Internet. Fragestellungen, Modelle, empirische Befunde*. München (Verlag Reinhard Fischer).

Stallings, W. 2003. *Cryptography and Network Security*. Upper Saddle River, New Jersey (Pearson Education, Inc.).

Winkel, O. 1999. "Die Förderung von Vertrauen, Glaubwürdigkeit und Verläßlichkeit. Welchen Beitrag kann die elektronische Verschlüsselung dazu leisten?" In: Rössler/Wirth (Hrsg.) 1999. Pp. 193-208.

Towards an Understanding of the Psychology of Non-Photorealistic Rendering

NICK HALPER, MARA MELLIN, CHRISTOPH S. HERRMANN,
VOLKER LINNEWEBER, THOMAS STROTHOTTE

Abstract

This paper proposes the necessity of developing a theory of psychology within non-photo-realistic rendering (NPR). Despite the inherent flexibility of NPR within a variety of visual media, the psychological functionality of NPR remains largely unexplored. As such, we consider aspects of NPR in terms of general, biological, social, and environmental psychology paradigms using results from recent studies, while discussing options for further research and applications.

Introduction

Although psychological research into virtual realities (Bente, Krämer, & Petersen, 2002) and visualization techniques (Bullinger & Ziegler, 1999; Forsythe, Grose, & Ratner, 1998) continues to increase, and growing technical developments and applications further support advances in photorealism (PR), the psychological potential of non-photorealistic rendering (NPR) remains largely a *terra incognita*. Therefore, within the broader framework of establishing an interdisciplinary focus on 3D-virtual worlds, this paper outlines the psychological fundamentals within NPR for both basic and applied research.

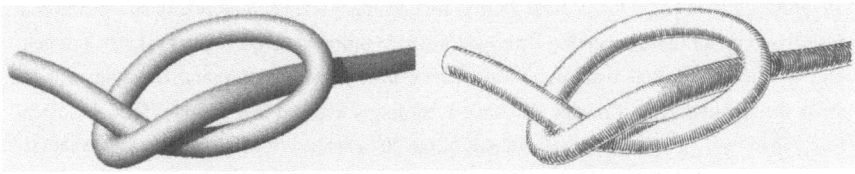

Figure 1: Examples of an image rendered using PR (left) and NPR.

Although the differences between the PR and NPR images within Figure 1 can be considered algorithmically (see, for example, Strothotte & Schlechtweg, 2002), the more fundamental question of differential use remains, particularly, variations of NPR styles considered according to various user contexts.

More specifically:

- Which emotions can different NPR images evoke?
- Which cognitive and/or neurophysiological processes are activated by differentially rendered images of the same object?
- How does NPR effect interaction with objects in user interfaces?
- How does user expectations effect object perception as a function of the image style?

As current research conclusions are quite limited (Schumann et al., 1996; Interrante, 1997; see also May, 2000), these questions remain very pertinent to NPR in its increasing technological capacity and consequent applications.

Although this paper discusses experimental results, we largely focus on theoretical concepts in terms of future work and interdisciplinary research. To begin, we concentrate on four areas accordingly: general psychology, social psychology, biological psychology, and environmental psychology in terms of research we conducted (Halper et al., 2003) with theoretical roots in early studies on visual perception of shapes (Provins, Stockbridge, Forrest, & Anderson, 1957; see also Ramachandran & Hirstein, 1999; Gooch, 2002), while considering NPR's applicability for participatory design (Schumann, Strothotte, Raab, & Laser, 1996) in future work as it applies to both NPR and psychology. After which, we briefly discuss an architecture for authoring tools for NPR and outline how the psychology of NPR could be embedded in such systems.

Psychology and Visualizing Reality

As the modern world develops and utilizes IT applications for work, communication, advertising, and play at an exponential rate, the subsequent demand for psychological research into human-computer interactions has emerged. Because IT interactions are particularly visual, much of virtual reality (VR) incorporates psychological paradigms of visualization (Bente et al. 2002) in addition to other technical developments and applications (Bullinger & Ziegler, 1999; Forsythe *et al.* 1998). Virtual worlds are becoming an everyday reality and therefore a research topic for those accepting Brunswik's (1955) proposal on ecological validity as a general orientation. Virtual realities are interactive in a more complex and multidimensional sense than many forms of media, and have accordingly evolved into a topic of psychological research in its own right in the second half of the 20th century. It may be anticipated that virtual realities will shift into the focus of an increasing variety of psychological research paradigms. Indeed, with the advent of avatar technology, the differentiation of reality and VR is becoming increasingly fuzzy (Schreier, 2002).

General Psychology

General Psychology is mainly concerned with behavior and cognition, and in terms of NPR, offers several relevant theories surrounding visual processing. Specific to our research of NPR, we discuss *figure-ground-segregation:* when lines, surfaces, and colors facilitate object identification relative to other objects within the visual field.

Figure-Ground-Segregation for NPR Guided Selection

When visual information increases in a given image or scene—as in PR environments, the probability for figure-ground segregation errors also increases. Therefore, homogeneously structured simple surfaces are easier to detect and identify as belonging to the same object (Hoffman, 1998), and therefore, rendering objects using defined 'figure' or 'ground' styles, enables the viewer to more rapidly and accurately assess the status of objects within a complex scene. Indeed, our results indicate that NPR styles can strongly facilitate figure-ground segregation processes. In a recent study Halper et al. (2003) asked subjects to "click on three objects" from a set of 20 objects. About half of the objects displayed were rendered in cartoon-style (strong silhouettes and two-tone shading), and the other half were rendered with the same oil-paint style used for the background (see Figure 2). Subjects were randomly assigned to one of two test conditions (A or B—as in Figure 2) to control for biasing based on object preference. Overall, subjects tended to select two or more cartoon-style objects, indicating that rendering style was a greater factor in selection choice than actual object attributes.

Figure 2: A magnified view from the Halper et al.'s interactive rendering task (2003). The left (test A) and right image (test B) use two different rendering styles (cartoon-style and oil paint) to 'define' objects as 'active' versus those perceived as part of the background or 'inactive.' Subjects shown the left image tend to select the active truck while subjects shown the right image tend to select the active duck.

Future Directions for NPR and General Psychology

Other general psychological theories such as prior knowledge, associative conditioning, and the geon theory are also relevant to NPR and future psychological research. For instance, *prior knowledge* can reinforce behavior in the guided selection of objects discussed above, such that repeated experiments coupled with consistent object interactions would likely strengthen the influence of rendering style until subjects cease to interact with background objects altogether. This could then be applied to interactive graphics, with the potential to simplify and guide user choice. *Associative conditioning* occurs when two or more elements or objects become associated because of an observed relationship (visuo-spatial, temporal, auditory etc.) between the assessed elements. Indeed, graded levels of active and inactive rendering styles associated with the functionality of objects may influence subject responses accordingly. Associations may also be formulated based on other NPR elements within the image. Lastly, the *geon theory* states that humans perceive objects using 'geons,' or compositions of the most elementary geometrical shapes. The simpler an object is, the fewer geons must be processed before achieving object identification, thus NPR images could support image identification when using simpler rendering algorithms relative to the number of geons necessary for image identification within PR.

Social Psychology

Social psychology studies interactions, communication, and information exchange and is thus relevant to NPR in a number of areas. Our research focuses on aspects of social perception and judgment.

Using NPR to Influence Social Perception and Judgment

Social perception and *social judgment* utilize learned values and behaviors to respond to socially ambiguous situations, wherein interpretation of other people and their expressions— verbal and non-verbal, are necessary (Bente & Krämer 2002; Dörner & Schaub, 2002). Simple optical elements may be used to evaluate a person or situation using stereotypic character attributions when too little explicit information is available. Within our own labs, assessments of safety and danger were influenced via line-style: subjects shown Figures 3 and 4 and subsequent variations tended to perceive the normal lines as safe (whether shown on the house or the tree), and the jagged lines on the door as dangerous. Moreover, images of a geometrically identical character using only variations in line strength successfully conveyed character strength and weakness, wherein subjects tended to assess the characters rendered with thicker, more solid lines as strong, and the sketchy, thin-lined characters as weak.

Figure 3: When asked to select the safest location, subjects choose the trees over the house rendered using jagged lines. In contrast, subjects presented the same house rendered using straight lines tend to regard the house as safer (Halper et al., 2003).

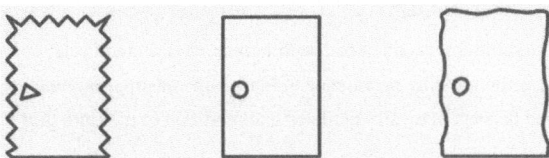

Figure 4: In identifying the door that contains danger,
most subjects choose the door on the left with jagged line styles (Halper et al., 2003).

Future Directions for Social Psychology and NPR

In terms of the research discussed above, more complex images, subtler test questions, and extended understanding of social judgments could provide definitive insights into how NPR can be used to guide and influence users and their perceptions of images and environments in general. Furthermore, NPR may also influence *aggressive* and *altruistic* behaviors. For example, NPR and social psychology would benefit from tests measuring the behavioral consequences of negative reciprocity (Felson & Tedeschi, 1993; Mummendey et al., 1984; Patchen, 1993) and whether they vary depending on how a character is rendered (strong, dangerous, etc.). These results might also extend Zimbardo's (1969) early studies on de-individuation, wherein aggressive, reckless, and chaotic behaviors increased in subjects when their identities were masked. Indeed, game environments might reveal much potential in these areas as online players frequently conceal or change their identities. It is possible that via rendering attributes, which convey more information about the player's behavior, certain negative behaviors would then decrease as a result of a sort of 'unmasking' that takes place when the player is no longer able to completely conceal negative aspects of their behavior. Lastly, game designers could systematically vary characters and scene presentation for their own utility within the game, or create 'game' programs employed towards both psychological and gaming goals to better understand the psychosocial impacts of the online game world.

The *minimal group paradigm* is concerned with minimizing errors of perception within inter-group relationships (Diehl 1990) by reducing the arbitrary influences that encourage false group identification (e.g. "All people wearing glasses are smart"). Within NPR, stimuli could be reduced to a minimum of necessary elements, thus decreasing the potential for arbitrary group attributions and identifications while furthering insights into social psychology. Lastly, effects of rendering parameters, such as color, may vary between cultures, whereas other aspects of rendering, such as the threat-connotative line styles (see Figures 3 and 4) are culture-independent. An analysis of how NPR can be used to convey messages across and within demographic groups could optimize user interfaces as well as help establish techniques for universal communication.

Environmental Psychology

Environmental psychology is concerned with human-environment relationships. Of particular interest to NPR, is the growing prevalence of human-media environment interactions, wherein environments can be systematically modeled and modified to measure user responses.

Participation and Interaction in Environments

NPR has long proven useful in the fields of architecture and urban planning: presentation techniques initiated by the Berkeley Environmental Simulation Laboratory (Appleyard & Craik, 1978) have been designed to improve user needs when viewing planning alternatives. Additionally, communication between experts and laymen has also developed due to improvements in CAD, visualization, and simulation (Linneweber, 1993). In terms of laymen— citizens, investors, and future users, participatory designs must facilitate interactions as well as basic design understanding. Schumann et al. (1996) demonstrated that NPR sketch-rendered design qualitatively improves the dialogue between architects and clients, in contrast with dialogues elicited from PR images. Psychologically, sketch-rendered designs maintain different affordances (Gibson, 1977; Munz, 1989), wherein sketched images appear preliminary, unfinished, and therefore open to change. Thus, the client is more likely to consider and suggest changes to the design.

NPR can also be employed to *guide* behavior. Halper et al. (2003) demonstrates that increased levels of detail (LOD) can effectively influence both navigation and exploration behaviors, wherein subjects asked to choose a path to explore or reach a goal in the distance (Figure 5), tend to select the path with the higher levels of detail. Potentially, subjects view increased LOD as more interesting for exploration, relative to lower LOD.

Figure 5: Implicit cues for exploration (left) and navigation (right).
Users tend to choose the detailed paths (Halper et al., 2003).

Future Research in NPR and Environmental Psychology

For interactive planning designs, tools may be developed that portray existing buildings as PR while using sketch rendering for structures under consideration. Indeed, this might be applied in a number of areas requiring feedback, wherein incomplete or unreliable information uses varying degrees of sketch rendering mapped to varying levels of certainty. For example, to encourage student participation via sketch rendered text and images within a lecture.

Further studies of exploration and navigation can by guided by NPR in conjunction with psychological theories: familiarity with a specific area may cued by decreasing LOD, while unknown areas maintain increased LOD to support spatial exploration behavior. For instance, the home range concept (van Vliet, 1983) demonstrates that human exploration patterns tend to resemble an ever-expanding circle, wherein space immediately next to the familiar locations is first explored until it becomes familiar before moving outward and so on. Combining experiments that encourage exploration based on visual stimuli could aid level-design to encourage viewers to explore particular areas. Unexplored areas in maps can be 'sketched', so that once explored they become more refined and 'finished.' A more precise evaluation of the interplay between LOD and sketched representations is necessary to understand how they might be used in combination.

Biological Psychology

Biological psychology is concerned with the relationships between behavior, cognition and concurrent brain processes—those relevant to NPR include feature binding, attention, and memory. *Feature binding* combines different visual elements (e.g. shape, size, and movement) to create a cohesive image(s) for identification and categorization ("that is a dog, he looks dangerous"). *Attention* occurs when sensory systems (visual, auditory, etc.) focus on certain stimuli, and can be automatically triggered (Wrigth, 1998) if certain criteria (e.g. relative size, shape, and newness) are fulfilled, thereby focusing attention on a given stimulus over other stimuli. Lastly, *memory* can influence attention and binding processes—effectively "tuning" individual binding processes to alter individual attention processes. Images already represented in memory usually require less attention because identification occurs rapidly, whereas new objects require increased attention before identification and categorization occurs. Moreover, the memory quality can influence attention, such that a negatively remembered object may increase attention over a new object.

Attention, Memory, and Binding

Relevant to the NPR research in Section 2, visual data can be "grouped" to deal with feature binding problems that may occur when the visual scene is too complex or "overloaded". Grouping images simplifies the scene, thus supporting feature binding in complex scenes via Gestalt rules of similarity. That is, if the different parts of an object(s) share the same qualities—in this instance, rendering style, it is easier for our brain to bind these parts together as a whole object or field of related objects. Thus, the toys rendered in the same style and separate from the background are perceived as such, whereas objects rendered in the same style as the background are perceived as belonging to the background. Moreover, processes necessary to figure-ground segregation discussed in Section 2 require increased levels of attention, such that those objects perceived as foreground necessarily receive more attention than those perceived as background.

Memory plays a central role in how images are visually perceived. Within our electroencephelogram (EEG) labs, increased brain activity occurs when subjects are exposed to new images (Herrmann & Bosch, 2001), indicating increased levels of binding and attention in order to categorize and respond to new images. Three images are displayed: the Kanizsa square (Figure 4, right), and a rotation of the elements constituting the Kanizsa square (Figure 4, left), wherein the subject must make a key-press with their left hand; while the third image (not shown) served as the target, which subjects respond to via a key-press with their right hand.

Figure 6: Kanizsa square (right) and control stimulus (left) demonstrate how memory representation results in differences in processing within the human brain.

Figure 7 shows the ERPs in response to Figure 6: subjects easily recognize the Kanizsa square within the negative space, while increased EEG activity for the second image indicates its perceived novelty. Moreover, the two images were identical in terms of brightness, contrast and only differ in a rotation of their elements. An ANOVA revealed that the Kanizsa square resulted in an enhanced N170 ($F(1,12)=7.28$, $p<0.05$). The N170 is a negative ERP component peaking at 170 ms after the image was presented on the screen. This indicates that the existing memory representation of a stimulus is evaluated by our visual system as early as 170 ms after presentation. Therefore subsequent processes of cognitive image processing will be influenced by the memory representation.

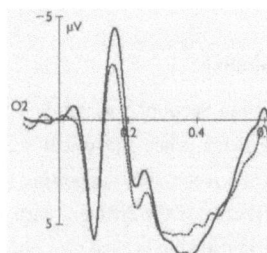

Figure 7: Event-related potentials at electrode O2 over human visual cortex show a difference between images for which subjects had a memory representation (solid line) as compared to an image that is new to subjects (dotted line). This difference appeared as early as 170 ms after the image was displayed on the computer screen.

Of particular interest to NPR, is the fact that memory seems to function independent of how realistic an image appears and has been demonstrated in infants as young as 11 months. When an object is new or implausible infants tend to attend to it longer than previously seen objects, while the duration of object fixation (or attention) is independent of how realistic or simplified the objects appears (cf. Figure 6) (Pauen, 2003). This suggests that NPR can effectively render objects and images in non-realistic styles without influencing primary feature binding processes necessary for basic object identification, while maintaining the potential to vary aspects of the identified objects in manners not possible within PR.

Figure 8: Realistic (top) and simplified (bottom) toy animals receive equal attention from 11-month infants.

Future Research in Biological Psychology and NPR

There is much potential for future research in biological psychology. Specific to our labs, we intend to combine EEG measures with assessments of safety based on rendering styles. It is possible that attention-related increases in brain activity will be observed for those objects rendered as dangerous. Within this paper, assessments of safety and danger have been considered in the context of social judgments, while Provin's radar research (1957) demonstrated that identification of triangles as foes and circles as friendly are pre-conscious processes. Consequently, such assessments of friend and foe could prove effective in facilitating character attribution via rapid character assessment within a game. Further research is necessary to elicit the extent to which triangulation of lines influences both pre-conscious and conscious assessments of danger and how these could respectively vary in terms of brain activity.

Furthermore, it is possible that neuropsychological research might uncover specific patterns of activity within visualization techniques using NPR variances in rendering in all the tests mentioned here. For example, interactive decisions regarding path exploration and navigation might reveal varying activation patterns dependent on such things as task, images, and the presence or lack of detail. Lastly, we plan to use an eye-tracking device to record eye movement from subjects exposed to mixed and independent PR and NPR images. Our hypothesis is that NPR and PR images will result in different observation times and eye movement patterns.

Perspectives

Currently, we are developing a software tool, OpenNPAR (see www.opennpar.org), which allows lay people, as well as programmers, to create new visual effects without technical knowledge of how the effects are generated. OpenNPAR is comprised of modules that can be fitted arbitrarily into a rendering pipeline, which then compute, based on known psychological effects of NPR, the presentation style most likely to achieve the desired effect, while mimicking a designer's creative process with a novel interaction method. Clearly, OpenNPAR stands in stark contrast to other rendering systems, which first demand the technical expertise to directly specify parameters in order to achieve the desired effects. Thus, all users—be they psychologists or computer scientists, can create effects to their own ends. Using this tool, psychologists are able to optimize experimental conditions for NPR.

Additionally, there are a number of important applications for software tools for NPR as just described. One of these is in the area of eBooks, which today offer little more than the possibility to browse in text. In order for eBook technology to be successful, an integration of images and text must first be enabled. Moreover, new interactive services must be offered that provide customized illustrations based on user input. Such illustrations will have to compete in quality with those in printed books, while flexibly adjusting LOD.

Applications of this technology could be utilized best in medical books for teaching and reference, as well as in technical documentation. Although these materials must be easy to use by end-users, it is equally important criterion that such a system is also easy for authors to utilize. Thus, the tool should adjust the renditions' style based on the effects the author wants to have on the end-user. The selection of styles must be carried out systematically and be based on empirical evidence as to the psychological effect of NPR on users.

In this paper we have (1) reported on recent results, which demonstrate that NPR can evoke reactions for which there are psychological explanations, and (2) outlined future directions for interdisciplinary research between psychology and NPR that will prove mutually beneficial, while providing tools in support of this marriage. Existing psychological paradigms can drive NPR, just as NPR can support future psychological experiments and research. The effectiveness of a particular NPR style can be evaluated via psychological measures ranging from statistical analysis of user selection to analysis of brain activity. As a result, known influences of NPR can be applied in virtual scenarios to optimize applications and testing conditions for psychological experiments. Although we are still far from a full theoretical account of the relationship between NPR and psychology, our recent research results are clearly suggestive of this interdisciplinary potential.

References

Appleyard, D., & Craik, K. H. (1978). "The Berkeley Environmental Simulation Laboratory and its research programme". *International Review of Applied Psychology, 27*, 53–55.

Bente, G., & Krämer, N. C. (2002). "Virtuelle Gesten: VR-Einsatz in der nonverbalen Kommunikationsforschung." In G. Bente, N. C. Krämer & A. Petersen (Eds.), *Virtuelle Realitäten* (Vol. 5, pp. 81–107). Göttingen: Hogrefe.

Bente, G., Krämer, N. C., & Petersen, A. (Eds.). (2002). *Virtuelle Realitäten* (Vol. 5). Göttingen: Hogrefe.

Brunswik, E. (1955). *The conceptual framework of psychology.* Chicago, IL: University of Chicago Press.

Bullinger, H. J., & Ziegler, J. (Eds.). (1999). *Human-computer interaction*, Vols. 1 & 2. Mahwah, NJ: Lawrence Erlbaum Associates, Inc., Publishers.

Diehl, M. (1990). "The minimal group paradigm: theoretical explanations and empirical findings." In W. Stroebe & M. Hewstone (Eds.), *European review of social psychology* (Vol. 1, pp. 263–292). Chichester: Wiley.

Dörner, D., & Schaub, H. (2002). "Die Simulation von Gefühlen." In G. Bente, N. C. Krämer & A. Petersen (Eds.), *Virtuelle Realitäten* (Vol. 5, pp. 57–79). Göttingen: Hogrefe.

Felson, R. B., & Tedeschi, J. T. (Eds.). (1993). "Aggression and violence: Social interactionist perspectives." Washington, DC: American Psychological Association.

Forsythe, C., Grose, E., & Ratner, J. (Eds.). (1998). *Human factors and Web development.* Mahwah, NJ: Lawrence Erlbaum Associates, Inc., Publishers.

Gibson, J. J. (1977). "The theory of affordances." In R. Shaw & J. Bransford (Eds.), *Perceiving, acting, and knowing* (pp. 67–82). Hillsdale, NJ: Lawrence Erlbaum.

Gooch, B. (2002): "Ramachandran and Hirstein's Neurological Theories of Aesthetic for Computer Graphics." *Siggraph Course Notes*, 2002, pp. 193–204.

Halper, N., Mellin, M., Duke, D., & Strothotte, Th. (2003). "Implicational rendering: drawing on latent human knowledge". submitted for publication.

Herrmann, C. S., & Bosch, V. (2001). "Gamma activity in human EEG is related to high-speed memory comparisons during object-selective attention." *Visual Cognition, 8(3/4/5)*, 593–608.

Hoffman, D. D. (1998). *Visual intelligence.* New York: Norton and Company.

Interrante, V. (1997). "Illustrating surface shape in volume data via principal direction-driven 3D line integral convolution." *Proc. SIGGRAPH*, ACM Press, pp. 109–116.

Linneweber, V. (1993). "Wer sind die Experten? 'User needs analysis' (UNA), 'post occupancy evaluation' (POE) und Städtebau aus sozial- und umweltpsychologischer Perspektive." In H. J. Harloff (Ed.), *Psychologie des Wohnungs- und Siedlungsbaus: Psychologie im Dienste von Architektur und Stadtplanung* (pp. 75–85). Göttingen; Stuttgart: Verlag für Angewandte Psychologie.

May, J. (2000). "Perceptual principles and computer graphics." *Computer Graphics Forum 19*(4), pp. 271–279.

Mummendey, A., Linneweber, V., & Löschper, G. (1984). "Aggression: From act to interaction." In A. Mummendey (Ed.), *Social psychology of aggression: From individual behavior to social interaction* (pp. 69–106). New York, NY: Springer.

Munz, C. (1989). "Der ökologische Ansatz zur visuellen Wahrnehmung: Gibsons Theorie der Entnahme optischer Information." *Psychologische Rundschau, 40,* 63–75.

Patchen, M. (1993). "Reciprocity of coercion and cooperation between individuals and nations." In R. B. Felson & J. T. Tedeschi (Eds.), *Aggression and violence: Social interactionist perspectives* (pp. 119–144). Washington, DC: American Psychological Association.

Pauen, S. (2003). "Denken vor dem Sprechen." *Gehirn und Geist, 1,* 45–49.

Provins, K., Stockbridge, H., Forrest, D., & Anderson, D. (1957). "The representation of aircraft by pictorial signs." *Occupational Psychology, 31,* 21–32.

Ramachandran, V., & Hirstein, W. (1999). "The science of art: A neurological theory of estheti experience." *Journal of Consciousness Studies 6*(6–7), pp. 15–51.

Rock, I. (1998). *Perception.* New York: Scientific American Books.

Schlechtweg, S., & Strothotte, Th. (1999). "Illustrative Browsing: A New Method of Browsing in Long On-line Texts." In *Human-Computer Interaction INTERACT '99*, pp. 466–473, Amsterdam –Berlin –Oxford –Tokyo –Washington, DC, 1999. International Federation for Information Processing, IOS Press.

Schreier, M. (2002). "Realität, Fiktion, Virtualität: Über die Unterscheidung zwischen realen und virtuellen Welten." In G. Bente, N. C. Krämer & A. Petersen (Eds.) *Virtuelle Realitäten* (Vol. 5, pp. 57–79). Göttingen: Hogrefe.

Schumann, J., Strothotte, Th., Raab, A., & Laser, S. (1996). "Assessing the effect of non-photorealistic rendered images in CAD." S.G.R. Bilger & M.Tauber (Eds.), *Proc. Computer Human Interaction* (CHI'96), pp. 35–42, ACM Press.

Sommer, R. (1983). *Social design. Creating buildings with people in mind.* Englewood Cliffs, NJ: Prentice-Hall.

Strothotte, Th., & Schlechtweg, S. (2002). *Non-Photorealistic Computer Graphics: Modeling, Rendering, and Animation.* San Francisco: Morgan Kaufmann.

van Vliet, W. (1983). "Exploring the fourth environment: An examination of the home range of city and suburban teenagers." *Environment and Behaviour, 15,* 567–588.

Wrigth, R. D. (1998). *Visual attention.* Oxford: Oxford University Press.

Zimbardo, P. G. (1969). "The human choice: Individuation, reason, and order versus deindividuation, impulse and chaos." In W. J. Arnold & D. Levine (Eds.), *Nebraska Symposium on Motivation* (Vol. 17, pp. 237–307). Lincoln, Nebraska: University of Nebraska Press.

Dynamic Visualisation for Feedback-driven Online Aggregation

ROLAND JESSE, GUNTER SAAKE, KAI-UWE SATTLER, THOMAS STROTHOTTE

Aggregation is generally a time consuming process only marginally suited for interactive result exploration. We present a framework of techniques to support an extended aggregation, which works online and can be controlled via user feedback. Supportive visualisation methods are presented with an overview of applicable interaction techniques and a generic architecture that combines relevant individual components.

1   Introduction

Data analysis scenarios are frequently challenged by questions about how best to properly represent and provide access to data sources. Aggregation is generally deemed a common basis for providing access to data objects, which maintain similar characteristics. Because aggregation is generally a time consuming batch operation, the development of online aggregation now provides better access to intermediate results, which are then gradually refined.

Following visualisation metaphors is one of a broad variety of visualisation techniques used to represent data to the user. Specifically, we are interested in an information landscape, which can dynamically map the currently available aggregation data onto geometric landscape objects, thus enabling adaptive visualisation to adjust to online aggregation. Given interaction methods for the information landscape, we are able to adopt a feedback-driven control of the online aggregation.

This paper is organised as follows: Section 2 introduces a component-based architecture for feedback-driven online aggregation, with further details outlined in Section 3. Next, Section 4 discusses the mapping process for creation of the landscape, while Section 5 covers dynamic visualisation techniques, which represent the online aggregation latencies. Finally, Section 6 presents interaction methods for aggregation feedback and Section 7 provides a summary and conclusion.

2   Architecture

A component-based architecture allows for various data sources to be aggregated, while applying information extraction operations, visualising the results, and provides user feedback for interacting with these processes. First, we outline a service-oriented view of this architecture, which describes the principle structure of the component composition and is followed by a more in-depth description of a client/server view of the architecture. Therein, a presentation client represents a generic visualisation application driven by a script-based visualisation description as generated by the server. This separation allows for multiple data analysis strategies to be employed alternatively.

2.1 Service-oriented view

A feedback-driven online aggregation system serves a service-oriented architecture, thus ensuring the integration of heterogeneous data with components for data analysis and manipulation. Following the design guidelines for an information fusion workbench by Dunemann et al. (2001), Figure 1 points out the interplay of separate services. A central *service registry* manages communication between the individual components. Each service is registered here and accesses all other services through the registry, thereby closely integrating each system component. The design of the registry follows the requirements for web-service components as described by Snell et al. (2002), which leads to an open interface–allowing for the integration of further components into the architecture itself, as well as the integration of this architecture or parts thereof into other systems.

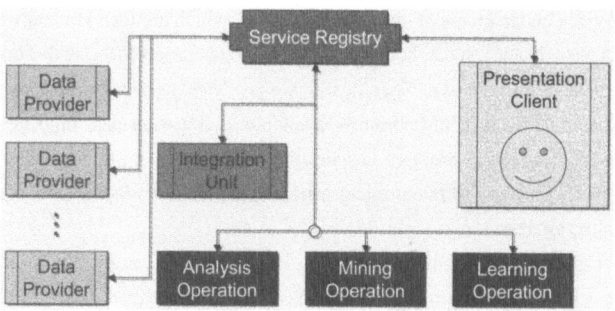

Figure 1: Service-oriented view of the architecture.

2.2 Client/server view

Figure 2 illustrates the physical separation of the components from Figure 1 into the client/server architecture necessary to generating presentations controlled by a script-based description. The client is used as the interface to the user and is responsible for the implementation of individual presentation techniques, while the server generates a visualisation description by mapping data onto geometry and constructs the script controlling temporal operation of presentation styles as described by Jesse (2003). Both client and server do not necessarily need to actually use the same computer as communication relies on a TCP/IP-based protocol.

Data integration and analysis components as described by Dunemann et al. (2002) are represented in the figure as the *data provide,* while the *geometry mapper* generates a geometric scene description of the aggregated data; an in depth discussion of this mapper is given by Jesse (2002). Section 4 discusses these architectural components in further detail. Finally, the *temporal mapping* and *interval mapping* components characterise visualisation helper functions thus controlling various aspects of graphics rendering while managing user events.

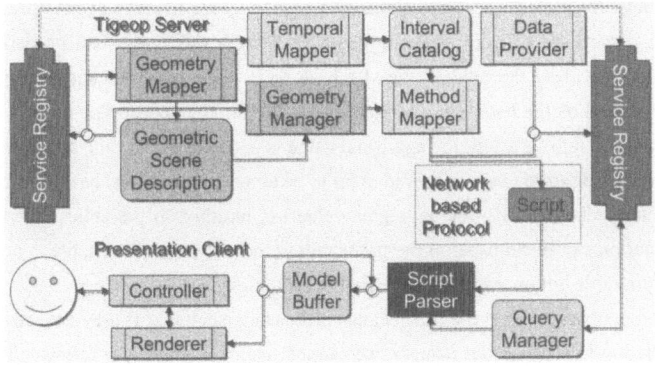

Figure 2: Overview of the script-based client/server architecture.

3 Aggregation

Data aggregation is one of the most important operations in many scenarios of data analysis and OLAP. Essentially, aggregation groups data objects according to a grouping criteria (such as equal attribute values) and computes an aggregate function on each group, ranging from simple functions such as *sum, average* or *min/max* to more complex statistical functions like *median, variance* and so on.

In today's database systems grouping and aggregation are performed typically in batch mode, i.e., first the whole dataset (relation) is processed before any result is given. This is mainly an attribute of the execution strategy: grouping is implemented generally confined to sorting, thus "blocking" the query pipeline. Although this is an efficient query plan, which minimises overall processing costs, it is not very well suited in scenarios with larger data sets where accuracy is not the predominant factor. In such cases, a better strategy would rapidly provide approximate results–further refining them as processing progresses. Moreover, not all results are necessarily of interest to the user. Therefore, an iterative refinement emphasising specific regions (groups) would effectively increase processing speeds of relevant groups.

In recent years, several approaches have been developed for *online aggregation* (Hellerstein et al., 1997; Haas and Hellerstein, 1999) that propose new operators guaranteeing nonblocking processing of queries. Obviously, online aggregation is restricted to operations which can be implemented without blocking. For instance, an ordered list of tuples cannot be computed in an online manner. A typical online query formulated in a hypothetical SQL dialect could be written as follows:

SELECT ONLINE x, y, AVG(z)

FROM dataset

GROUP BY x, y;

This means, for each group represented by a pair *(x, y)* the average of all values of the *z*-component is computed. In an online aggregation system this query can be performed by reading the tuples from the relation, build a hash table where each bucket corresponds to a group and—based on the hash value of the tuple—add it to the appropriate bucket. Each time a tuple is inserted into a bucket, the aggregate value is updated, i.e., for the above example we have to keep the *sum* and *count* values in order to be able to compute the average. At the same time the intermediate result—the aggregate value—is returned to the caller. Obviously, the result generation can be adjusted to the user's requirements, e.g. a result tuple is not returned for each input tuple but instead only for *n* processed tuples.

Another important issue is the order tuples processing, such that if they are retrieved from the base relation in a sequential manner, we cannot guarantee a uniform refinement of all aggregates. For example, if data are stored in a certain order of an attribute used for grouping, the first group (corresponding to the smallest attribute value) is finished before the computation of any other group can commence. Thus, the tuples should be retrieved in a random order or via a strategy fulfilling the user requirements (e.g., preferring certain groups). An appropriate strategy is overviewed in Section 6.

4 Mapping

There are a variety of techniques available to map data onto geometry representing data characteristics within specific application domains. Overviews of such techniques are presented by Schroeder et al. (1998); Schumann and Müller (2000); and Ware (2000). We do not intend to provide additional knowledge towards information visualisation techniques, but instead, propose to target a general description of methods for the representation of aggregated database content. For this purpose, a landscape metaphor is used, wherein all data is mapped onto objects forming a landscape, which is built on a formal information model, thus generalising the applicability of the presented techniques.

4.1 Information model

The design of the visualisation framework is formally based on the model presented by Kreuseler and Schumann (2002), which was developed in the context of Visual Data Mining, although it also allows for application in other domains. In principle, the model is based on the definition of *information objects* IO_i that combine to an *information space* $\mathbf{IM} = IO_1, ..., IO_n$ with $IO_i = IO_j \Leftrightarrow i = j$ and $i, j, n \in \mathbb{N}$. Each information object represents some real world data. In order to parameterise these objects according to their represented data characteristics, an attribute function *attr* is provided: $\mathbf{AM} = attr(\{IO_1, IO_2, ..., IO_n\}) = \{A_1, A_2, ..., A_k\}$ with $A_i = A_j \Leftrightarrow i = j$ and $i, j, k, n \mathbb{N}$. Thereby, $\mathbf{AM}$ is the *attribute set* of the respective information objects. For the purpose of defining relations between IO_i the *information structure* $\mathbf{IS}$ is introduced as $\mathbf{IS} \subseteq \mathbf{IM} \times \mathbf{IM}$.

4.2 Landscape construction

According to the information model, all information objects IO_i are described by an attribute set $\mathbf{AM}$ consisting of k attributes. All attributes $A_1, ..., A_k$ describe an information object in its information structure $\mathbf{IS}$.

Individual types of the attributes include their position according to the landscape coordinates, the height of a landscape object, its material information, and rendering style information. An information object IO as described by $A_1, ..., A_k$ is positioned as a cuboid on a two-dimensional landscape grid which is described as $\mathcal{L} = \{p_0, \vec{d_x}, \vec{d_y}\}$. Therefore, the landscape consists of an origin p_0 and two vectors spanning the x and y coordinate axis, respectively. The height and material attributes of information objects represent attributes of the respective data sets as retrieved in the aggregation process.

Figure 3: Landscape snapshots. The leftmost image represents a landscape without any mapped data. The remaining images show the representation of an increasing amount of mapped data.

Resulting screen-shots of a constructed landscape are shown in Figure 3. From left to right, the images represent increased availability of data as retrieved from a DBMS, wherein the information set $\mathbf{IM}$ is initially empty while individual information objects IO are added with increased data availability.

5 Dynamics for latency representation

Static images do not necessarily provide enough expressive power to represent the dynamic nature of latencies resulting from online aggregation. Therefore, we evaluate the potential of motion to enrich expression capabilities, thereafter we briefly discuss hybrid style combinations that preserve positive motion characteristics.

5.1 The value of motion

Motion is relatively easily for a user to perceive—demanding little cognitive input, before perception occurs. An early study by Johansson (1964) points out that changes in two dimensions are easily perceived as motion in 3D, that is, different frequencies in the x and y-directions of a stimulus pattern allow for perception of motion in the z-direction. Although this cognitive conclusion follows certain restrictions (such as velocity), it provides rich expressive capability as demonstrated in user studies (Bartram, 1997a,b; Ware et al., 1999), which were ultimately utilised by Bartram (1998, 2001) to enrich information visualisations with motion.

Despite the potential for motion to be used as a display dimension, actual implementation necessitates further questioning and subsequent restrictive guidelines. Pylyshyn et al. (1993) demonstrates that "it is possible to track about 4 randomly moving objects and to keep them distinct from visually identical distracters, such that events taking place on the tracked targets can be quickly detected and identified" (Pylyshyn et al., 1993, p. 21). This considerably confines motion techniques that might be employed simultaneously in a scene. Although the authors loosen the fixed limit of four objects, wherein five or fewer items can be cued from among a larger set, such that the cued items are then treated as though they were the only ones in the scene (ibid.).

Harrison (1995) reveals a more functional flaw in using motion to convey information: animations within an online help system—utilising both animated visuals and still graphics, was unable to provide either significantly more information or a more sustainable learning experience. These results are somewhat questionable as the animations within in the study were segmented to emphasise each stop of a procedural task. That is, the task at hand was not specifically designed to benefit from animated assets in the help system. Moreover, Morrison et al. (2000) furthers the limitations of animation in a literature review of user studies targeting the perception of animation. In most cases, animations were relatively ineffective because they are difficult to perceive or mismatch the user's conception of motion, which are often discrete rather than continuous.

5.2 Layered styles

The conception of dynamics by use of combined (layered) rendering styles directly follows the above doubts about the explicit use of motion. It is furthermore motivated by the classical design role that asks for the simplest possible presentation in order to communicate a goal and to gain a sustainable learning experience by the user (Dwyer, 1978).

Figure 4: Rendering of a landscape with hybrid styles as presented by Jesse and Isenberg (2003). The different styles emphasise possible delays in data retrieval as caused by the DBMS. The leftmost image shows an initial data set. The remaining images represent the addition of context data whereby the initial set is still visible. The styles for this initial set and the remaining scene are gradually combined and finally form the representation shown in the rightmost image.

Figure 4 applies hybrid-rendering styles to the landscape visualisation for the purpose of latency representation. Any possible delay in the retrieval of aggregated data is mapped onto the attribute set **AM** of currently investigated information objects $IO \in$ **IS**. As outlined by Jesse and Isenberg (2003), multiple rendering styles are then combined as a hybrid composition. Selected attributes $A_m, ..., A_n \in$ **AM** with $1 \leq m, n \leq k$ (cf. Section 4) are used to parameterise the respective rendering style, including—but not limited to: line style, line thickness, texturing, and colouring.

In order to connect the current status of aggregated data retrieval, rendering parameters are selected, which produce partially incomplete images, and are then gradually refined. If all data is finally and completely retrieved, results are derived from a single homogeneous rendering style.

6   Interaction for feedback

There are two principle restrictions for interaction support in online aggregation: handling of incomplete data sets and control of further aggregation processes. In order to comply with these system challenges, a selective overview of focus and context techniques is presented. We arrange these techniques in an interactive layer model to better illustrate their application potential in aggregation control.

6.1 Focus and context techniques

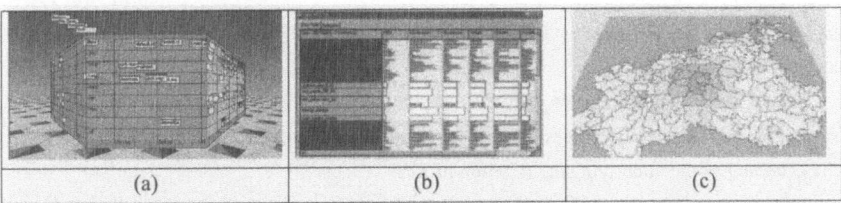

Figure 5: Focus & context techniques in visualisation systems. Subfigure (a) shows an exemplary *Perspective Wall* presentation (Spence, 2001, p. 117). An example of a *Data Table View* from Kreuseler and Schumann (2002) is displayed in (b) whereas (c) shows the location of spatial context of area neighbourhoods as outlined by Schumann and Kreuseler (2003).

Figure 5 presents a set of focus and context techniques. The *Perspective Wall* by Mackinlay et al. (1991) is a bifocal display which bends the presentation plane (Spence and Apperley, 1982), thus providing more information in space by focusing largely on the specific area of interest, while the rest of the scene is scaled down,.

The *Data Table View* by Kreuseler and Schumann (2002) is an extension of the *Table Lens* by Rao and Card (1994). Both techniques further the classic data table systems (Eick, 2000), such that the focused table area is magnified while minimising the remaining table contents.

Schumann and Kreuseler (2003) introduce the spatial context presentation of area neighbourhoods as seen in Figure 5(c) by following a landscape metaphor, wherein a specific data set is presented with varying context information allowing the centre of interest to be specifically highlighted and interactively changed.

6.2 Interaction layer model

The existing interaction techniques for online aggregation feedback can be employed at multiple levels of influences. Figure 6 presents a classification model wherein different interaction methods are respectively mapped onto visual feedback techniques and aggregation control, such that visual feedback is employed solely as a communicating system response to the user, surviving independently of aggregation controlling feedback processes.

Picking a specific object is equivalent to *selection* of this object for further aggregation. The complete set of classic presentation variables can be employed for emphasising the specific information object in question. Enhanced focus and context techniques such as the Data Table View do not provide valuable visual feedback regarding the singularity of the *IO* of interest. Using an *interaction lens* provides not only a singular information object, but also a set of n related objects with a context area ε. Although a single cursor does not suitably represent selection, the techniques presented above can. Motion, as visual feedback can be restricted to local animations to avoid referencing irrelevant information.

Although bending the presentation plane, as in the case of the Perspective Wall, is not appropriate for the landscape metaphor, other focus and context techniques supported by the bifocal concept are applicable. For example, fish-eye lens techniques (Sarkar and Brown, 1994) provide greater presentation space by shrinking non-focus areas instead of bending them away.

This lensing interaction layer allows for the selection of a set of information objects while restricting this selection to a specific area, thus the layer is specifically available to influence the *grouping* of the underlying aggregation process.

Lensing constraints are addressed at the *area selection* layer, allowing not only one object or area to be selected but also multiple information sets **IM**, such that the cursor for visual feedback is only used for single selections. In contrast to the lensing layer, motion for feedback can now be applied globally to express the identity of selected areas via similar motion techniques, thus allowing this layer to combine the control capabilities of both alternative layers within the aggregation processes.

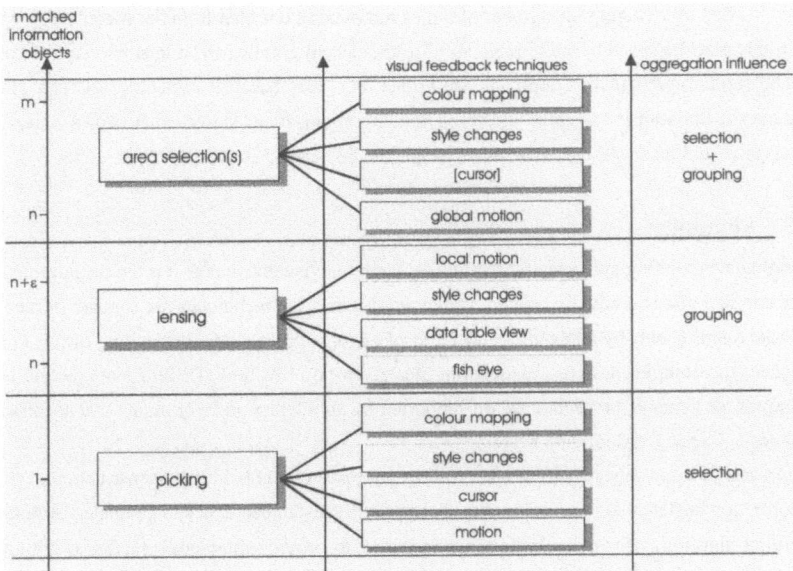

Figure 6: Interaction layer model. Different interaction techniques provide respective feedback possibilities for online aggregation control by accessing respective sets of information objects.

6.3 Query refinement and aggregation control

A feedback mechanism is necessary to react to the selection of a given interest in the scene by changing the speed of the aggregation of the associated groups. This can be achieved by adjusting the strategy for fetching tuples from the base relation. However, this requires information about the group memberships of the tuples: in this case we are able to fetch more tuples from the focused groups than from others.

One approach is to exploit index structures such as bitmap indexes which are commonly used in data warehouse environments. Assuming indexes defined on the grouping attributes we can identify the members of a group simply by looking at the index. Based on this, feedback-driven online grouping/aggregation can be performed as follows:

1. The number of groups and the grouping values are obtained from the index.
2. The different groups are aggregated in a round-robin manner. Starting with the first index value (representing the first group), the first corresponding tuple is read, the hash function for grouping is applied and the tuple is "added" to the appropriate group.

Then, a tuple from the second index value (corresponding to the second group) is retrieved and so on.

3. If the user focuses on a certain group (or several groups) the retrieval strategy is modified by changing the number of tuples retrieved in one step from the specified group.

In this way the speed of the refinement of user-selected groups can be interactively increased. The shortcomings of this approach are higher I/O costs because switching between groups makes it impossible to exploit clustered storage organisation. However, it allows a more interactive and feedback-driven analysis which can be beneficial in many applications.

7 Summary

Online aggregation puts specific requirements onto a visualisation as it provides intermediate result data that is gradually refined. Dynamic visualisation techniques are capable of meeting these requirements by adjusting to latencies of aggregated data while providing means to represent the completeness of a data set at any given point in time. Different interaction techniques for dynamic presentations are supported by an interaction layer model that specifically takes online aggregation into account.

Clearly, these concepts are subject to ongoing research, including the construction of transformation buffers that provides on-the-fly access to pre-fetched data and geometry. Automatic filling algorithms for these buffers are expected to provide interactive access to arbitrarily large data sets. Possible application domains therefore include data warehouses and virtual communities.

References

Linda R. Bartram. Perceptual and Interpretative Properties of Motion for Information Visualization. Technical Report CMPT-TR-1997-15, School of Computing Science, Simon Fraser University, 1997a.

Linda R. Bartram. Can Motion Increase User Interface Bandwidth in Complex Systems? In *Proceedings of 1997 IEEE Conference on Systems, Man and Cybernetics*, pages 1686-1692, 1997b.

Linda R. Bartram. Enhancing Visualizations With Motion. In *Hot Topics: Information Visualization 1998*, pages 13-16, North Carolina, USA, 1998.

Linda R. Bartram. *Enhancing Information Visualization with Motion*. PhD thesis, Simon Fraser University, 2001.

Oliver Dunemann, Ingolf Geist, Roland Jesse, Gunter Saake, and Kai-Uwe Sattler. InFuse – Eine datenbankbasierte Plattform für die Informationsfusion. In Andreas Heuer, Frank Leymann, and Denny Priebe, editors, *Datenbanksysteme in Büro, Technik und Wissenschaft, BTW 2001*, pages 9-25, Oldenburg, 2001. Springer.

Oliver Dunemann, Ingolf Geist, Roland Jesse, Gunter Saake, and Kai-Uwe Sattler. Informationsfusion auf heterogenen Datenbeständen. *Informatik, Forschung und Entwicklung*, 17(3):112-122, September 2002.

Francis M. Dwyer. *Strategies for Improving Visual Learning*. Learning Services, 1978.

Stephen G. Eick. Visualizing Multi-Dimensional Data. Computer Graphics, pages 61-67, February 2000.

Peter J. Haas and Joseph M. Hellerstein. Ripple Joins for Online Aggregation. In Alex Delis, Christos Faloutsos, and Shahram Ghandeharizadeh, editors, SIGMOD 1999, Proceedings ACM SIGMOD International Conference on Management of Data, pages 287-298, Philadelphia, Pennsylvania, USA, 1999, ACM Press.

Susan M. Harrison. A Comparison of Still, Animated, or Nonillustrated On-Line Help with Written or Spoken Instructions in a Graphical User Interface. In I.R. Katz, R. Mack, L. Marks, M.B. Rosson, and J. Nielsen, editors, *Proceedings of the ACM Conference on Human Factors in Computing Systems*, pages 82-89, ACM, 1995.

Joseph M. Hellerstein, Peter J. Haas, and Helen J. Wang. Online Aggregation. In Joahn Peckham, editor, *SIGMOD 1997, Proceedings ACM SIGMOD International Conference on Management of Data*, pages 171-182, Tucson, Arizona, USA, 1997. ACM Press.

Roland Jesse. Motion enhanced Information Mural for Climate Data Visualisation. In Konrad Wojciechowski, editor, *Proceedings of the International Conference on Computer Vision and Graphics (ICCVG 2002)*, volume 1, pages 374-379, 2002.

Roland Jesse. Script-based presentation of simulation results. In Thomas Schulze, Stefan Schlechtweg, and Volkmar Hinz, editors, *Simulation und Visualisierung 2003*, pages 441-452, Magdeburg, March 2003. SCS-European Publishing House.

Roland Jesse and Tobias Isenberg. Use of hybrid rendering styles for presentation. In Vaclav Skala, editor, *Poster Proceedings of WSCG 2003*, 2003.

Gunnar Johansson. Perception of motion and changing form. *Scandinavian Journal of Psychology*, 5(3):181-208, 1964.

Matthias Kreuseler and Heidrun Schumann. A Flexible Approach for Visual Data Mining. *IEEE Transactions on Visualization and Computer Graphics*, 8(1):39-51, January-March 2002.

Jock D. Mackinlay, George G. Robertson, and Stuart K. Card. The perspective wall: Detail and context smoothly integrated. In *Proceedings of the ACM Conference on Computer Human Interaction: CHI'91*, pages 173-180, 1991.

Julie Bauer Morrison, Barbara Tversky, and Mireille Betrancourt. Animation: Does It Facilitate Learning? In Andreas Butz, Antonio Krüger, and Patrick Olivier, editors, *Proceedings of Smart Graphics*, AAAI 2000 Spring Symposium Series, pages 53-60. AAAI Press – American Association for Artificial Intelligence, 2000.

Zenon W. Pylyshyn, J. Burkell, B. Fisher, C. Sears, W. Schmidt, and L. Trick. Multiple parallel access in visual attention. *Canadian Journal of Experimental Psychology*, 1993.

Ramana Rao and Stuart K. Card. The Table Lens: Merging graphical and symbolic representations in an interactive focus+context visualisation for tabular information. In *Proceedings CHI'94*, pages 318-322. ACM, 1994.

Manojit Sarkar and Marc H. Brown. Graphical Fisheye Views. *Communications of the ACM*, 37(12):73-84, 1994.

Will Schroeder, Ken Martin, and Bill Lorensen. *The Visualization Toolkit – An Object-Oriented Approach to 3D Graphics*. Prentice Hall PTR, 2. edition, 1998.

Heidrun Schumann and Matthias Kreuseler. Fokus&Kontext-Darstellungen im geographischen Kontext. In *Proceedings of GeoVis 2003*, 2003.

Heidrun Schumann and Wolfgang Müller. *Visualisierung*. Springer-Verlag, Berlin Heidelberg New York, 2000.

James Snell, Doug Tidwell, and Pavel Kulchenko. *Programming web services with SOAP: building distributed applications*. O'Reilly, 2002.

Robert Spence. *Information Visualization*. Addison-Wesley, 2001.

Robert Spence and M.D. Apperley. Data Base Navigation: An office environment for the professional. In *Behaviour and Inforamtion Technology*, volume 1, pages 43-54, 1982.

Colin Ware. *Information Visualization: Perception for Design*. Interactive Technologies. Morgan Kaufmann Publishers, 2000.

Colin Ware, Eric Neufeld, and Linda R. Bartram. Visualizing Causal Relations. In *Proceedings Information Visualization 1999*, San Francisco, USA, 1999.

The Representation of Shape for Retrieval of Pictures by Semantic Means

KLAUS-D. TOENNIES, KLEMENS BÖHM, CHRISTOPH S. HERRMANN, INGO SCHMITT

Abstract

Content-based image retrieval (CBIR) allows the user to search an image database via image features rather than keywords. Although database search techniques are relatively advanced, CBIR systems remain limited in their ability to close the gap between search semantics and the potential of their translated features. Thus, a deeper understanding of object search and recognition behaviours, as well as those object features necessary for defining image representations, will advance and supplement CBIR systems in effectively extracting and integrating semantic information via user feedback during the search process.

Introduction

The concept of a content-based image retrieval (CBIR) system has existed for about 10 years with the intention of easing database indexing—a tedious and error-prone task [Bess1990], by utilizing image features (see [Velt2002] for a current evaluation of 58 CBIR systems). Effective CBIR systems must accurately represent both objects and abstract concepts in pictorial form, using only a specified array of pixels, intensity, and colour features.

This paper explores CBIR in terms of the complex relationships between picture features as expressed within the image representation in order to more directly map attributes to their represented features, thereby narrowing the gap between search semantics and the potential of their translated features.

Content-Based Image Retrieval

Eakins et al. [Eaki1999] identify three types of requests in their review of state of the art CBIR:

- **Primitive requests** using data based features such as histograms, colour distributions, or texture features for finding similar images. A search of this kind could identify images containing a blue region in the upper third of the picture, as there is no differentiation between differing semantics within this region.
- **Semantic requests** require that image features be combined with a-priori-knowledge regarding how features may be interpreted within the context of the request. For example, a successful database search for a picture containing mountains first necessitates pre-existing information about how the mountains are mapped into the image.

- **Abstract requests** search for abstract entities expressed within the image, such that the picture is merely an exemplified mapping of the entity. Such a search might seek images that express romantic feelings.

Thus, a request in CBIR is not posed in terms of the image itself, but rather a representation of related image features that are frequently represented by a feature vector, wherein quantifiable attributes such as histograms of colour, grey scale, or texture features are entries of the feature vector. Moreover, features may be weighted and the weighting may in turn change during the search. An image search then becomes a task of identifying locations in feature space where the requested picture might found, and can be further specified by giving positive or negative feedback regarding previously found pictures.

Currently, a majority of CBIR systems solely address *primitive requests*, and are able, for instance, to search for images of a given colour and/or texture distribution, as any system, being automatic or feedback-driven can only make a request in terms of those features immediately represented or derived from a given image. Features contained within *abstract* or *semantic* requests maintain a particularly indirect relationship with their respective sought-after object attributes.

A mapping of semantics onto, say, a mountain and its primitive features (e.g., colour distribution) will be inevitably fuzzy. However, such features are easy to generate and feedback regarding image relevance can enable the user to identify arbitrary locations in feature space, after which, feature weights can optimise the request in terms of these extracted features. Feedback then provides a-priori-knowledge necessary to semantic and abstract requests. Even so, the relation between semantic features (attributes of a mountain) and primitive features (distribution of colours and/or textures) remains relatively ambiguous. Indeed, primitive feature values can have multiple meanings (blue could be sky or water), while an object may be pictured in multiple ways. This incongruity is known in the CBIR community as the *semantic gap*, and can be safely assumed to increase relative to the distance between semantic and primitive features. Thus, there is no certainty that all pictures containing the desired object can be found, as the primitive feature value combinations may not be identified. Furthermore, images containing different objects with similar feature values may not always be properly differentiated.

Shape and Visual Perception

Image features used for picture retrieval are often too simple for describing the semantics of a request via the image representation alone, as retrieval systems assume that a combination of such features will describe concepts with higher semantics despite the fact that the features may not. While this is true in some cases, it is may not actually be possible to combine desired features such as local colour or texture distributions to uniquely represent a specific meaning; and even when it is possible, small perturbations in image features such as shading may cause the features to no longer represent the desired object, although the picture continues to depict the desired object.

Ideally, the expressive power of a feature-based representation of image content should be directly related to the request meaning, unfortunately this would make the request dependent solely on image content. For instance: an appropriate representation of mountain features in an image would be derived from our knowledge about how mountains are mapped into pictures, while it may be of little use to deduce perceptually similar images depicting different objects (e.g., different types of mountains). Therefore, it is helpful to have an object-independent representation serving as a container for image attributes deemed to be relevant for describing similarity. User input can then teach specific cases of perceptual similarity representation. In the example above, this means that a possibly complex similarity criterion for mountains is developed through user feedback on retrieved images. However, such relevance feedback can teach similarity only in terms of a pre-defined similarity measure on the representation of image features.

Current picture descriptions frequently employ the above-mentioned simple features grouped into a vector, from which a (weighted) norm is defined in terms of similarity. Of all the different primitive features, shape is actually used the least in content-based image retrieval, although it can be characterised fairly easily as the outline of a structure, because it is difficult to represent shape in a manner that allows perceptually similar shapes close to each other to be based on some distance metric in feature space. On the other hand, shape is clearly an important feature for describing and differentiating objects in pictures. Indeed, humans perceive only certain details in pictures that automatically 'grab' our attention [Para1998]. Furthermore, features that are remembered are influenced by picture context [Ande1995]. Even at 8 months, electrophysiological responses can be measured in infants when they perceive 'good' shapes or shapes following basic Gestalt laws of grouping [Csib2000].

If pictures are to be retrieved from a database according to image content, it is important that the user can employ picture criterion that tend to be both perceived and remembered. Indeed, the human processing of pictorial information requires that pictorial components be combined to create a coherent object representation [Herr2001]. Thus, the representation extracted from the picture must be first, capable of representing shape, colour, texture and so on, as well as the extent to which these features and objects containing them, actually coincide with existing knowledge regarding perception and perceptual similarity.

A second key consideration for CBIR systems is the process of specifying a request by the user, with existing CBIR systems requests typically (1) posing query images, (2) directly adjusting feature values such as colour distribution, or (3) sketching query images. However, the complexity and increased informational demand of shape retrieval necessitates an adequate query language using a declarative first-order-logic-based language (similar to domain calculus in RDBS) basing on a set of predefined similarity predicates in correspondence to specific shape features. Due to similarity values, Boolean junctures would need to be replaced with fuzzy-operations, while weighting atomic search terms could differently enhance the expressive power to respond more precisely to user needs (see [Schu03]), and query weights would be reasonable parameters for relevance feedback cycles.

The representation of shape

If shape is a container for knowledge taught by user feedback, then it must incorporate an indepth understanding of the relationship between perceptual similarity and shape. Because image analysis regarding 2-D and 3-D shape representations are used for classification purposes and CBIR may be viewed as a classification task, the following considers how shape representations (although only 2-D are used, most conclusions are extendable to 3-d representations) should be in some way deformable in order to enable them to adapt generic shapes to given shapes within the image. Within the recent past, various deformable shape models have been developed for use in segmentation, motion tracking, reconstruction, and shape comparison, which can be broadly classified into three classes:

- **Statistical models** using a-priori knowledge regarding shape variation in terms of shape reconstruction
- **Dynamical models** fitting shape to the data via built-in smoothness constraints for an optimal solution
- **Structural models** extracting structural features from shapes for comparison and classification

Statistical models are best represented by Active Shape and Active Appearance Models as developed by Cootes et al. [Coot2002], which utilize principal component analysis in order to describe variations of landmarks and textures. Another candidate is the probabilistic registration by Chen [Chen1999], which employs the per-voxel gray level and shift vector distributions to guide a better fit between a grey-level atlas representing expected image content and the data, while smoothness constraints between neighbouring shift vectors improve the results. Although statistical models describe the statistical variations of a fixed-structure shape, they fail to account for structural differences between different shapes. For instance, if an object consists of two parts, this fact is not described in the representation although the shape of this object may be represented. Moreover, if a part is missing then this may be read as a mere deformation of the representation, which would have the same quality as a deformation of one of the parts (e.g., due to measurement errors) although the perceptual difference may be much greater. Without this missing part the shape may even be a different object altogether.

Examples of *Dynamical Models* are: the front propagation methods of Malladi et al. [Mall1995] using an expanding closed curve that eventually fits the shape; or Szeliski et al.'s [Szel1993] dynamic models, which simulate a system of dynamic oriented particles expanding into the object surface guided by internal forces that maintain an even and smooth distribution between them. These deformable models are able to segment and sample objects of complex topology like blood vessels, with the central restriction in their lack of statistical or structural shape characterisation. Within a CBIR system, a shape may be found in the image given enough support from the data but without incorporating a similarity measure into the representation. These kinds of representations are more suitable for finding—rather than classifying shapes.

The shock grammar by Siddiqi et al. [Sidd1996] or the finite element method of Pentland et al. [Pent1996] are both *Structural Models*. The shock grammar defines four types of shocks or evolving medial axes formed from colliding propagating fronts that originate at shape boundaries, with restrictions on shock type combinations for shape formation, wherein grammar eliminates invalid shock combinations. The shock graphs describing a shape facilitate comparisons between shapes. The method of Pentland et al. defines a dynamic finite element model for shape fitting such that the low order modal coordinates describe the object structure under its free vibration modes: a simple dot product of the modal vectors of two shapes is a strong discriminator of their structural differences. Other related examples of shape representation are the super quadrics by Terzopoulos et al. [Terz1991] or shape blending by DeCarlo et al. [DeCa1998]. All of these models are data driven in that they have no prior knowledge regarding fitted shape structures. Although this is advantageous for CBIR shape representation in that object information can be incorporated through relevance feedback, shapes are not described statistically, thus making a similarity measure difficult to install.

A partial solution is found in the active structural shape model [AlZu2002], which combines aspects of the structural model with the ability to represent and learn statistical shape variations from the dynamic model. However, even this representation is not able to learn structural features for classification.

A representation for shape-based CBIR

At present, no existing shape representation meets all of the demands of a CBIR system, although there exists clear potential to fulfil at least some of the properties. Ideally, a shape representation in CBIR should have the following features:

- A shape representation generated from an existing picture should be a combination of an object classification by shape and variations due to measurement or other permissible variations, while facilitating the separation of these different aspects. Structo-statistical representations could be a suitable solution as structures are mainly class-specific whereas statistical variations reflect shape changes due to permissible object variations.
- Shape features should be adaptable to specifications from user feedback such that it agrees with knowledge about perceptual similarity. In other words, foreseeable groupings by the user are accounted for according to Gestalt laws and are reflected in higher-level features of the shape representation.
- Shape should be separable into structural units that may be influenced by neighbouring units or underlying structural units, while separate treatment of the shape units by

user request should be possible for enabling independent similarity measures for different parts of the shape description. For example, a tree remains a tree if some branches are missing but not without a trunk.

- Topological and geometrical variations of a shape representation are separable. Admittedly, this requirement is challenging, as many shapes can be thought of a geometric deformation of some base shape or a construction of different topological units. Specifically, the cipher 3 can be thought of as a deformation of a line or the combination of two cups and depending of application, either of the two representations may be the more appropriate as defined by the user request and learned from feedback.

A shape representation maintaining the above properties would provide a container for user input based on user perceptions of shape, such that the request is both more precise and goal-oriented than one based on more primitive shape features. However, features of such complexity can no longer be represented as a simple vector of values, as structural relationships, topological and geometrical properties and a hierarchy of shape will constitute the shape description. Clearly, new learning methods as well as appropriate similarity measures must be further explored.

Conclusions

The potential of CBIR is far-reaching in a highly visual and technologically dependent society where the ability to produce pictorial information currently far exceeds the ability to retrieve this information. CBIR attempts to free the image-gathering user from the task of retrieving images based on a pre-specified description of content via a general content-based search. However, understanding of the relationships between image content and image information representation remains unsatisfactory at best as automatically generated representations of an image do not possess enough expressive power to accommodate user input with a specific content during the image search. Developing an in-depth understanding and an appropriate representation requires interdisciplinary research within human image interpretation, database management, and computer vision in order to effectively and algorithmically describe human perception in terms of image processing during the search an image database.

References

[AlZu2002] S. Al-Zubi, K.D. Toennies. Extending active shape models to incorporate a-priori knowledge about structural variability. LNCS, Vol.2449 (*Pattern Recognition, 24rd DAGM Symposium*), Springer-Verlag, 2002, 338-344.

[Ande1995] J.R. Anderson. Cognitive psychology and its implications, New York: W.H. Freeman, 1995.

[Bess1990] H. Besser. Visual access to visual images: the UC Berkeley image database project. Library Trends, Vol. 38(4), 1990, 787-798.

[Coot2001] T. Cootes, C. Taylor. Statistical Models of Appearance for Medical Image Analysis and Computer Vision. Proceedings of SPIE (Medical Imaging 2001: Image Processing), Vol. 4322, 2001, 236-248.

[Chen1999] M. Chen. 3-D Deformable Registration Using a Statistical Atlas with Applications in Medicine. Proc. MICCAI, 1999, 621-630.

[Csib2000] G. Csibra, G. Davis, M.W. Spratling & M.H. Johnson. Gamma oscillations and object processing in the infant brain, Science 290(5496), 2000, 1582-1585.

[DeCa1998] D. DeCarlo, D. Metaxas. Shape Evolution with Structural and Topological Changes using Blending. IEEE Transactions on Pattern Analysis and Machine Intelligence, Vol. 20(11), 1998, 1186-1205.

[Eaki1999] J.P. Eakins, M.E. Graham. Content-based image retrieval: A report to the JISC technology applications programme. 1999, http://www.unn.ac.uk/iidr/report.html.

[Herr2001] C.S. Herrmann, A.D. Friederici. Object processing in the infant brain, Science, 292, 2001, p.163.

[Mall1995] R. Malladi, J. Sethian, B. Vemuri. Shape Modeling with Front Propagation: A Level Set Approach. IEEE Transactions on Pattern Analysis and Machine Intelligence, Vol. 17(2), 1995 158-175.

[Para1998] R. Parasuraman. The attentive brain, Boston: MIT press, 1998.

[Pent1996] A. Pentland, R. Picard, S. Sclaroff. Photobook: Tools for content-based manipulation of image databases. Intl. J Computer Vision, 18(3), 1998, 233-254.

[Schu03] N. Schulz, I. Schmitt. Relevanzgewichtung in komplexen Multimediaanfragen. Datenbanksysteme für Business, Technologie und Web, LNI P-26, 2003, 187-196.

[Sidd1996] K. Siddiqi, B. Kimia. Toward a Shock Grammar for Recognition. IEEE Conf. on Computer Vision and Pattern Recognition, 1996.

[Szel1993] R. Szeliski, D. Tonnesen, D. Terzopoulos. Modeling Surfaces of Arbitrary Topology with Dynamic particles. Proc. Computer Vision and Vision Recognition (CVPR), 1993, 82-87.

[Terz1991] D. Terzopoulos, D. Metaxas. Dyanamic 3D Models with Local and Global Deformations: Deformable Superquadrics. IEEE Transactions on Pattern Analysis and Machine Intelligence, Vol. 13(7), 1991, 703-714.

[Velt2002] R. Veltkamp, R. Tanase. Content-Based Image Retrieval Systems: A Survey. Tech. Report. Department of Computer Science, Utrecht University. 2000, (revised version 2002) http://give-lab.cs.uu.nl/cbirsurvey.

Specialisation in Media Technology at the University of Rostock

RENÉ ROSENBAUM, HEIDRUN SCHUMANN, RAINER KOHLSCHMIDT

In response to the growing demand for educated professionals focusing on multimedia related industry, the University of Rostock developed a new specialisation in *media technology* in 1995. Although the engineering department at the university has long conducted research regarding the organisation, processing, transmission, and representation of multimedia data, these issues are now formally covered in lectures and coursework offered by various faculty within the engineering department.

The media technology specialisation is a joint effort of both the *Telecommunications and Information Electronics* (ET&IT) and *Computer Science* (CS) departments with additional contributions from the departments of law and philosophy. The multifaceted lectures provide students opportunities to increase not only their technical knowledge of multimedia, but overall media competence. The necessary intermediate diploma is finished within one of the above two departments, which then determines the department from which a Masters of Science may be completed, that includes a media technology specialization certification.

Media technology lectures include the following topics:

- **Basics**:
  Theoretical basics to application and use of media
    o Media Theory I and II (offered by the department of philosophy)
    o Media Law I and II (offered by the department of law)
- **Basics of Circuitry and Signal Theory** (offered by ET&IT):
  Theoretical basics to design and structure of electrical circuits and systems
    o Electronic devices and circuits I and II
    o Basics of Communications Engineering I and II
    o Signals and Systems I and II
    o Digital Signal Processing I and II
- **Device and process engineering** (offered by ET&IT and CS):
  Introduction of hardware for media processing
    o Audio- and Video technique
    o Computer Graphics hardware
    o Multimedia architectures
- **Transmission and storage of media streams** (offered by ET&IT and CS):
  Handling of general media data in various environments
    o Communications Systems I and II
    o Java and Web technology
    o Internet protocols and services
    o High-performance and mobile networks
    o Multimedia databases

- o   Information systems and services
- **Creation of media and Computer Graphics** (offered by CS):
  Specialized lectures to images regarding the creation of content
    - o   Basics of Computer Graphic
    - o   Realistic image rendering
    - o   Geometric modelling
    - o   Physically based modelling and animation
    - o   Visualization
    - o   Aspects of Computer Graphics
- **Design and processing of media streams** (offered by ET&IT and CS):
  Specialized lectures to the handling and manipulation of images
    - o   Image processing
    - o   Image compression
    - o   Multimedia communication
    - o   Computer Vision I and II
    - o   Dialog systems and software ergonomics

Although all existing forms of media can not be taught in depth, media technology lectures do cover a markedly wide spectrum, with more specific seminars offered by partners from the Institute for New Media, the ANOVA Multimedia Studios and the Fraunhofer IGD Rostock.

Currently, computer science students specialising in media technology can independently select the above lectures with certain regulations: a minimum of 20 hws (hours per week/semester) are to be attended covering a given subject, with a minimum 4 hws of subject *basics*. Additionally, 16 hws are dedicated to computer graphics with at least 8 hws of electives—(e.g. *transmission and storage of media streams*). Except 8 hws within the main course, all offered lectures can be freely chosen. This flexibility is further supplemented by the fact that lectures can be substituted rather easily, and depending on administrative rulings, even updated, adapted and changed. Lastly, although the department of Telecommunications and Information Electronics has slightly different curriculum regulations, the overall structure is quite similar.

Although the exact number of students specialising in media technology is not yet available due to a lack of statistics in combination with current students not being required to announce their specialisation before they are finished, informal feedback indicates that media technology is accepted as a valid specialisation.

To avoid overlapping lectures, the media technology lectures are fitted independently into each departmental time tables, and any resulting overlaps are then removed. Moreover, the media technology specialisation is considered in one of our post-graduate programs, the "Graduiertenkolleg", which brings together post-graduate students from different departments to combine their specialized work in interdisciplinary efforts. Every student within the program attends a minimum of 4 hws in media technology lectures, thus increasing their breadth of extra-disciplinary knowledge and opening new synergistic research opportunities.

Alumni job opportunities, though not limited to, include the following:

- the rapidly growing field of new studio techniques (radio and TV), especially within the upcoming digital audio and video systems,
- the use and development of an increasing number of multimedia techniques directly relevant to small and medium-sized companies.

Clearly, there are opportunities in *every* field where digital media is used or might be supportively employed such as publishing and news agencies.

Conclusion

The *media technology* specialisation now offered by the University of Rostock, educates a new breed of specialists in an ever-expanding field, involving many departments and partners in the wide-spanning theoretical and practical curriculum. Despite the many departments involved, media technology has been effectively integrated into the overall course structure, thus allowing the specialisation to remain relatively flexible in its orientation. Additionally, media technology lectures are used within our post-graduate program to enable further interdisciplinary work. Finally, student feedback indicates that the media technology specialisation is both widely accepted and viewed as a valuable contribution to furthering the education of skilled labourers in multimedia technology.

An examination of the use of Web-based Resources in an on-site M.Sc. Course in Multimedia Technology

IAN J. PITT

Abstract

This paper describes the experiences of staff at University College, Cork, Ireland, in designing and developing an extranet and courseware system to support the M.Sc. course in Multimedia Technology in the Computer Science Department. Although developed in consultation with both students and staff, the initial system achieved only limited success and has largely been abandoned. This paper examines some possible reasons for this lack of success and considers their implications for the design of future systems.

Introduction

In October 1999, University College Cork introduced a M.Sc. course in Multimedia Technology. A few third-level institutions in Ireland had already introduced multimedia-related courses, and most of the remaining institutions have since followed suit.

The range of postgraduate multimedia courses on offer from third-level institutions is quite diverse. They can be broadly categorised as follows:

*	Applications-based courses, on which students learn general principles (concerning design, colour, etc.) and the use of applications such as Photoshop, Illustrator, Director, etc. Most such courses are open to both arts and science graduates.
*	Technology-based courses, on which students learn about the theoretical principles and underlying technology (hardware and software), but only incidentally about the use of applications. Such courses generally require a first degree in a science or technology subject.

The M.Sc. Multimedia Technology course at UCC was designed as a technology-based course. Building on existing skills within the Computer Science Department, the initial curriculum included web-programming, graphics programming, virtual-reality, digital video, and digital audio, as well as graphical design and print-based technologies. Unlike many other multimedia-related courses then in existence, great emphasis was placed on the teaching of programming/scripting languages and skills. The range of languages taught included Java, JavaScript, Python, XML, PHP and VRML.

The M.Sc. in Multimedia Technology was originally conceived as a multi-track course, catering for students from both arts and science backgrounds and leading, via various optional modules, either to an M.A. or an MSc. It is still hoped that this model may one day be fully implemented. However, the availability of government grants for science courses – coupled with the relative lack of grants for arts courses – suggested that it would be easier to attract students onto a science course. Therefore it was decided that, initially at least, the course should be offered as a M.Sc. that could be taken by both arts and science graduates.

This created a number of problems. The most serious was that, while science 'conversion courses' for arts graduates exist in Ireland, they normally lead to a Higher Diploma rather than a masters degree. There was considerable resistance to the idea that arts graduates could be taught a science-based subject to masters degree level in one year, the normal period for a masters degree program. The alternative – extending the course to two years – was rejected on the grounds that it would deter many applicants.

The result was a compromise – a masters degree programme with a fairly intensive teaching schedule that ran nominally for 15 months, but with an option to complete the final project in a shorter period and finish after 12 months.

A further problem was the number of students taking the course. Government funding was sought and obtained, providing a quota of funded studentships for the course. The quota was set at 60, and pressure was exerted on the course organisers to fill this quota. Thus the course started with 60 students, drawn from a very wide range of backgrounds.

Use of the Web

From the outset, web-based teaching was encouraged and used, for the following reasons:

*	It was hoped that placing material on the web would enable students to study at their own speed outside lecture hours, thus helping those with less technical backgrounds to keep up with the teaching.
*	It was felt that a multimedia course, covering many web technologies, should be taught in a manner that reflected its content.

In line with this approach, modules on web-programming were taught with the aid of web-notes that included working examples of JavaScript, XML, PHP, etc., while the Java graphics course made extensive use of applets.

Although it was always intended that web-based resources should be used where possible, there was little attempt to coordinate their use or define goals or a strategy. Since no external assistance was available for the preparation of teaching materials, the level of provision depended upon the skills and knowledge of individual lecturers. This led to wide variation in levels of provision, with pressure being placed on those who made least use of the web to provide a similar level of support to that offered by their colleagues.

In the summer of 2000, with the first group of students moving onto the project stage of the course and a new student intake due in the autumn, the use of web-based resources was reviewed. It was noted that the students had expressed strong support for the use of web notes and interactive web-based teaching materials, but had voiced dissatisfaction with the variation in levels of support. It was also felt that there were opportunities to improve delivery of the course, and particularly assessment, through greater use of the web.

Design of the Courseware System

A survey was carried out in order to determine what changes should be made to the existing facilities, and what new facilities should be added. Commercial and other existing courseware solutions were examined in order to produce a list of possible components, and the list was then augmented with suggestions from staff and students.

The survey was carried out using two online form-based questionnaires: one for the lecturers and one for the students. The surveys left room for students and lecturers to make their own suggestions. Respondents were invited to rank the usefulness or likely usefulness of both existing and potential facilities.

When all the results were collected 50% of the full-time students had replied and 80% of the lecturers. Thus the total sample was 25 students and 4 lecturers.

Once the surveys had been analysed, a list of recommended features for a new courseware system was drawn-up. The list was as follows:

*	An Assignment Submission and Reporting Tool
*	A Calendar
*	A Link Management System - a system that allows students to submit the URLs to various online resources that they thought might be of use to their classmates.
*	Course Material Database
*	Bulletin Boards
*	A Resource Booking System - a system that could be used by staff and students to reserve workstations and equipment for certain time slots and if possible allow for block booking of the same time over a number of weeks.
*	A Student Notice Board

Some of these components were suggested by students, by means of the survey and follow up interviews, after the initial list was drawn up. Further details of the survey and its analysis can be found in Russell et al. (2003).

Implementation

There was no external and limited internal funding available, so the system had to be developed from scratch at little or no cost. This automatically precluded the use of software learning systems such as Blackboard or WebCT.

The obvious solution was to use open source software. As there was no one open source product that provided all of the required services, each component part of the system had to be approached separately. A set of criteria were drawn-up for each component, after which potential open source solutions were examined to see if they provided the functionality required. Those that met the requirements were modified to fit into the system and to create the impression of a seamless product.

The final choices are listed below.

Calendar: Matt Kruse's Calendar CGI Perl Script (http://www.mattkruse.com/scripts/calendar) because, through evaluation of code and testing, this script proved to meet all the criteria.
Link Management: Links v2.0 (http://www.gossamer-threads.com/scripts/links/index.htm). This system was free for non-profit use and met all the criteria.
Course Material Database: Links v2.0 was used for this component also. It allows lecturers to keep course material on their own servers (or any other server) and simply add links via the administration page of the links database. The links database allows for any kind of URL to be added, so it is also be possible to link to PDF files, graphics, QuickTime movies, etc. This offered flexibility for Multimedia staff whilst offering a uniform, structured interface for the students.
Bulletin Board: "The Ultimate Bulletin Board", developed by the Infopop Corporation in Seattle, Washington, USA (http://www.infopop.com). This met all the criteria. This system was already in use within the university so it cost us nothing to use.
Resource Booking System: the CALBOOK system, developed by Jan Snellman in the Department of Mathematics in Stockholm University (however, for various reasons this facility was never fully implemented - see Russell et al., 2003)
Student Notice **Board:** a Perl script and an HTML form were used to provide this functionality
Assignment Submission: It was concluded that there was no product or single piece of code that met the specific criteria laid out for the Assignment Submission and Report-

ing Tool and therefore a system must to be built from scratch. This was written in PERL and provided the following functions:

Assignment Creation – When a lecturer set a new assignment for his/her module, they were also able to use the Assignment Submission and Reporting Tool to name the assignment and give it a due date so that students could submit their homework to it.

User Management – The system had a user management facility. Staff could add, edit and delete new student users as well as new staff users.

Secure Upload Facility –This system allowed individual users to be assigned specific directories to upload their files to.

Reporting Facility – The system included a method for showing which students had handed in their work and when.

Experiences in the First Year and Beyond

The system was finished and ready for use when the second student intake arrived at the beginning of October 2000. It was used by all the lecturers and students throughout the following year, although not all lecturers used all the facilities. It was noted that enthusiasm for the system waned over time, with some lecturers using it only for a limited range of tasks (e.g., making lecture notes available to students) while others made extensive use of web-based resources but did so without using the courseware.

The look and feel of the site began to fragment over the year as individual lecturers (most of whom had considerable web design experience) began to modify the templates in order to suit their own requirements. This led to the use of different navigation systems for different parts of the site, and as a result, the cohesive nature of the site began to deteriorate. This, combined with a disinclination on the part of some lecturers to maintain certain areas of the site meant that large areas of it fell into disuse and as a consequence students began to lose interest in using the site.

By the following academic year, the only parts of the site that remained in use were some of the original page layout templates. Lecturers continued to place teaching materials on the web – indeed, the quantity and variety of material placed on the web increased significantly – but most did so independently of the courseware system.

Analysis

Despite the limited success of the courseware, there is still considerable enthusiasm for eLearning among the multimedia students and staff. Student surveys – carried out each year since the course started- invariably praise the use of web-based teaching materials and demand more rather than less web-based teaching. However, lecturers complain that producing high-quality web-based teaching materials is extremely time consuming and is only possible if time can be saved in other areas of course administration and delivery. This, of course, was one of the aims of the courseware system, but it seems to have failed in achieving this aim.

The limited success of the courseware system has prompted multimedia teaching staff to look again at the issues. In particular, staff are debating the role of web-based teaching and how it should be combined with traditional teaching in the delivery of on-site courses. This debate is taking place as other departments within UCC begin to consider the use of eLearning, and in some cases turn to multimedia teaching staff for advice.

It seems clear that one major problem is a mis-match between the needs of students, the needs of lecturers, and the practical constraints of time, resources, etc.. The courseware system took into account the opinions of both students and lecturers, but failed to ensure that (e.g.) facilities demanded by students could be delivered by lecturers within the available time and resources.

To be effective, eLearning systems must balance the needs of students and teaching staff, and also take into account the practical limitations of software, network infrastructure, etc.. However, research suggests that many current programmes are 'media-centered', i.e., institutions purchase software packages such as Blackboard, and then base their eLearning programmes around the capabilities of the software rather than the needs of students and/or staff.

The courseware system was designed to meet the (perceived) needs of multimedia students and staff, and thus cannot be described as 'media-centered'. A number of institutions (mainly large US Universities) have taken a similar approach, developing software tools that are tailored (through surveys, feedback-forms, etc.) to the needs of staff and students. However, the resulting systems usually require enormous staff resources and thus do not offer a practical model for most third-level institutions.

The importance of balancing the needs and capabilities of students, teaching staff and resources is now generally recognised, but there is little consensus as to where the balance lies. The trend in much recent research present has been to identify a balance for a specific course (Sangra et al., 2001), but this offers only limited guidance to those planning other types of course.

A more fundamental problem is that the site was designed with no clear pedagogical aims, other than that greater use of web-based material was desirable and that use of the web for assessment and project submission, etc., might ease administrative overheads.

The use of web-based resources in distance learning has been extensively investigated. However, the use of similar tools in 'Blended Learning' – i.e., teaching that involves both e-Learning and traditional, face-to-face teaching – is still poorly understood. A few Blended Learning courses have been examined by researchers, but many of these are closer in style to distance-learning courses than traditional face-to-face courses (e.g., part-time programs taught mainly over the web but with a short residential element, such as that described in Dean et al., 2001). Moreover, the huge range of possible 'blends' means that few of the research results can be generalised to other courses.

It is also unclear whether what generally passes for eLearning – placing course materials on the web with the aid of tools such as WebCT and Blackboard – significantly affects student learning (Epper & Bates, 2001). Thus there is a strong possibility that much effort is being expended to little effect. This is particularly worrying since it is generally agreed that the preparation of eLearning materials requires more time and resources than is needed in traditional teaching (Bonk, 2002). Despite the apparent enthusiasm of students for more web-based teaching, there is a risk that inadequately-planned adoption of eLearning might reduce the staff time available for traditional teaching whilst offering few if any benefits, thus lowering teaching standards.

There is also anecdotal evidence that encouraging the use of eLearning alongside traditional teaching without providing clear guidelines leads to widely-differing levels of implementation, and confusion among students. A wide variety of approaches can be observed among colleagues here and in other institutions: some lecturers place copies of their lecture-slides on the web, some use the web solely to distribute material not covered in lectures, and some adopt an approach somewhere in between (e.g., placing outline notes on the web and augmenting these with examples, etc., during lectures). Feedback from students suggests that they frequently fail to notice differing approaches to web-use unless these differences are extreme or are made explicit. Thus they tend to assume (for example) that if Lecturer A states that his/her entire course is on the web, then the material on Lecturer B's web-site must also cover his/her entire course.

It is also widely believed among lecturers (although not documented, to the best of the author's knowledge) that providing high quality online materials leads to lower attendance at lectures. This is not necessarily a problem, provided the online material is designed to cover the entire course. However, this brings us back to the purpose of the lectures: if the entire course is presented online, perhaps the time otherwise devoted to lectures can be used more effectively to enhance learning rather than merely duplicating the online material.

Conclusions

Despite the problems described above, there is good reason to believe that eLearning can deliver benefits, if properly implemented. Various studies have shown that appropriate combinations of traditional teaching and eLearning can improve students' performance. For example, Dean et al. (2001) tested students before and after taking a number of course modules and compared the improvement in performance across the modules. They found no significant difference between modules that used online learning and those that were taught using traditional approaches; however, some modules that used the two approaches in combination produced results significantly above the average. Other studies have suggested that drop-out rates can, in certain circumstances, be reduced through the use of eLearning (Stanford University EPGY, 2001).

The challenge is to determine the factors that produced success in these particular cases and to find ways of adopting them to suit new and existing programmes.

References

Effectiveness of Combined Delivery Modalities for Distance Learning and Resident Learning; Dean, P., Stahl, M., Sylwester, D. & Peat, J. (2001), Quarterly Review of Distance Education, July/August 2001

Teaching Faculty How to Use Technology: Best Practices from leading Institutions, Epper, R.M. & Bates, A.W. (eds), Oryx Press, 2001, ISBN 1-57356-386-2

Online training in an online world, Bonk, C. J. (2002), Indiana University, Bloomington, IN/CourseShare.com.

Developing Courseware for an on-site M.Sc. Course in Multimedia Technology, Russell, G., Pitt, I.J. & Couse, G. (2003), accepted for presentation at the Informing Science + IT Education Conference, to be held in Pori, Finland, June 24-27th 2003 (http://is2003.org/)

Putting the Student first: When an Innovative Model Leads to a New way of Learning, Sangra, A., Duart, J.M. & Guardia, L. (1999), proceedings of the Fifth International Conference on ALN, www.aln.org.

Development of a Master's of Science Degree within Multimedia Management

GERHARD WEBER

1 Introduction

From 1967 when Douglas Engelbart developed the mouse to the present, user interfaces have developed exponentially, and with the arrival of bitmap displays and the popularity of graphical user interfaces, object-oriented programming is now a core paradigm of user interface development. Nowadays collaborative systems use distributed system techniques while applying methods from Human Computer Interaction to identify tasks and the content of use.

However, the speed of knowledge increase in processing and generation of pictorial and acoustical presentation, as well as synthesis of forces for haptic sensations in multimodal user interfaces incorporating deixis has to be balanced with the need for designing applications of multimedia such as in education, entertainment, and business.

In 2001, the Universities of Kiel, Christian-Albrecht University, University of Applied Sciences and Muthesius-Hochschule (Academy for Art and Design) formed a common board to establish a private/public partnership for post-graduate education, research, and development in the domain of Multimedia and E-Business. Below, we discuss the integration of ongoing research projects concerning the Master's of Science in Multimedia Management.

2 The Degree

The Schleswig-Holstein's government has clearly identified the need for qualified computer science graduates able to combine experiences in media design with management of multimedia project resources. Recently in Kiel, an award-winning post-graduate degree program was formed, which emphasizes the combination of multimedia and eBusiness. Graduate profiles are based on their previous degree in combination with:

- skills in selected topics of media informatics including object-oriented programming, operating and database systems
- competence in management of an eBusiness via eProcurement, eMarketplaces, as well as eShops
- experience in the production of audiovisual media
- knowledge in basic concepts of media aesthetics and design

Students from any discipline can be admitted into the twelve-month program provided they have an above average degree and demonstrate their qualifications within an interview. The interview screens student's existing knowledge in IT, management, and fluency of English as all courses are taught in English, thus allowing qualified international students to study at the MMC. Although, mainly German students were enrolled during the first academic year of the program, this ratio has since inverted to include a majority of international students. Indeed, very little of student work is written in German, except for the thesis itself. Moreover, international students make good use of the compulsory language courses in German.

2.1 Studying at MMC

The MMC academic year began with top representatives from supporting organisations speaking at the commencement ceremonies. Teaching selection is independent of the University's system, with courses defined by quarters, which allows students to cover 90 ECTS each calendar year. Although, students are told to prepare for courses beginning in October, a few preparatory math courses are offered in September. Several scholarships covering tuition fees are available to both German and international students. Although vacations are infrequent and prolonged periods of illness are difficult to make up, the MMC administration is flexible if exam regulations allow for a second chance. However, a failed second exam during the first quarter leads to expulsion from the program.

The MMC is supported by the likes of the Ministry for Science, Ministry for Economy, the city of Kiel, the chamber of commerce Kiel, and by Technologie Stiftung Schleswig Holstein. Frequently, organized events such as a brown bag lunch with the minister of economics and open house days, allow MMC students to informally meet company representatives. Indeed, local industry offers projects for industrial placement of students during the last quarter of the academic year when they are writing their thesis, which can cover topics relating to:

- media production in business TV or sound design in live recordings etc.
- visualization of business processes in eBusiness
- media informatics (e.g. interactive TV services from XML mark-up to XSLT).

Upon completion of their thesis, students are ceremonially awarded bilingual certificates, while the best student and best Master's thesis are also formally recognized.

2.2 Curriculum

The curriculum is based on modules as listed in Table 1. All students enrol in courses that cover the three modularised principles of media informatics, administration/management, and media design. At the end of the first quarter, students select one major module.

Module	Weekly hours/ quarter (QWS)
Principles of Media Informatics	18
Principles of Business Administration/Management	14
Principles of Media Design	16
Media Informatics Major	36
E-Business Major	31
Communication Design Major	35
Master's thesis	21

Table 1: Modules in the degree program

Table 2 outlines the courses within the major modules *media design* and *media informatics*. Coursework is highly integrated with lecturers, such that focus (for example) on eShop, management of website development, requirements analysis, object-oriented programming and database normalization are all taught at different levels within various courses. Another core didactic chain leads to competence in mark-up languages—beginning with elements of coding theory and standards for movie files, and looks at HTML and CSS, Chomsky grammars, XML-based servlet programming for client/server architectures, and TopicMaps as an example of semantic Web technology.

Modules	QWS
Principles Media Design	16
Media Design I	4
Media Esthetics	4
Media Technology	4
Media Law	4
Media Informatics Major	36
Object Oriented Programming	6
Computer Graphics	6
Distributed Systems	6
Multimedia User Interfaces	6
Media Design II	6
Software Engineering	6

Table 2: Courses in Modules related to Media Informatics

The Blackboard learning platform (see Figure 1) maintains a web-based repository of teaching materials—providing both contact during industry placement and alumni access to teaching material. Moreover, the eLearning platform increases exposure to other Christian-Albrecht University courses and thus, the collaborative potential between CAU and MMC.

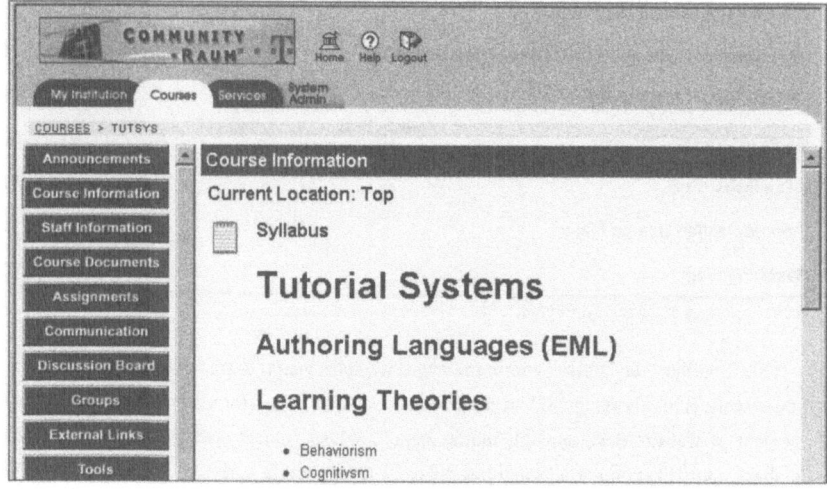

Figure 1: Bilingual eLearning platform

Courses range from classic lectures during the first quarter to team-oriented developments in the third, while web-based collaborations with lecturers and mentors provide students with extra and time-saving support.

Regular evaluation of each course and a number of proposals has led to a major re-working of the exam regulations after the first academic year in 2001/2002 and allows now adaptation of the study program to student's interest during the third quarter.

2.3 Faculty and structure of MMC

Currently, the permanent faculty are: the Chair of E-Business, CAU Dept. of Social Sciences and Business Studies and the Chair in Human Centered Interfaces, CAU Dept. of Technology, with additional professors and assistant professors from the Institute of Informatics at CAU, as well as lectures conduct at the Musthesis Academy.

The structure of MMC (see Figure 2) illustrates how closely related it is to its founding bodies: the "Förderverein", which consists of representatives of regional industry, works jointly with the "Förderstiftung" board consisting of, among others, the rectors of the Kiel universities and the mayor of Kiel.

Several externally and internally funded research projects are ongoing at MMC including:

- KOGGE project for entrepreneurship[1]

---

[1] http://www.uni-kiel.de/kogge

- Ph.D projects, and
- EU-Project MultiReader

The following describes research questions and preliminary results of the MultiReader project.

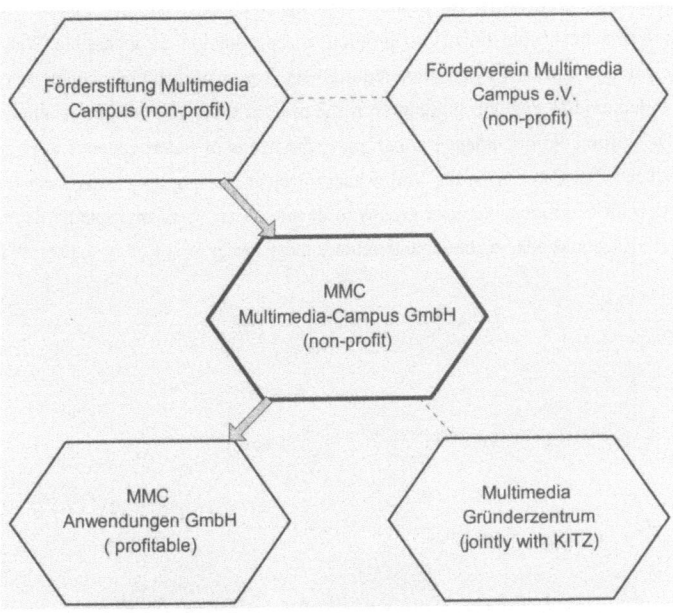

Figure 2: Structure of Multimedia Campus

3 EU Project MultiReader

Multimedia documents are more popular than ever with increased computer storage and bandwidth for transmission of information via the Internet and mobile telephones, wherein increasingly complex images, text, videos and animations has facilitated an increased spread of multimedia, with both advantages and disadvantages for print-disabled people: those with visual, auditory, mental, or physical disabilities that make print documents difficult to handle. On the one hand, it is easier than ever to manipulate text—converting it into speech, replacing it with graphics, and other options which make multimedia documents more accessible to print-disabled readers. But if multimedia documents are not constructed to be accessible to print-disabled readers, these advancements simply become another barrier for them.

Although there are now pre-established fundamentals necessary to making information accessible to print-disabled people, there are several complex issues, such as how they can navigate through multimedia and hypermedia documents. Currently, the EU-funded MultiReader Project is exploring how to best produce multimedia documents in an efficient manner that meet the needs of a wide range of print-disabled readers and particularly their navigational needs. One method to achieve this might be the development of guidelines, such as the Web Content Accessibility Guidelines 1.0 produced by the Web Accessibility Initiative of the World Wide Web Consortium (W3C) to promote the production of accessible Web sites. However, we contend that the navigational requirements for print-disabled people are not yet sufficiently understood to develop guidelines at the present time. In addition, it remains unclear just how multimedia documents, which meet the needs of heterogeneous user groups, are to be produced. For that reason the MultiReader Project is using an iterative user-centred design process with heterogeneous user groups to develop a series of multimedia documents such as tour guides, cookbook, art book, and explore these issues.

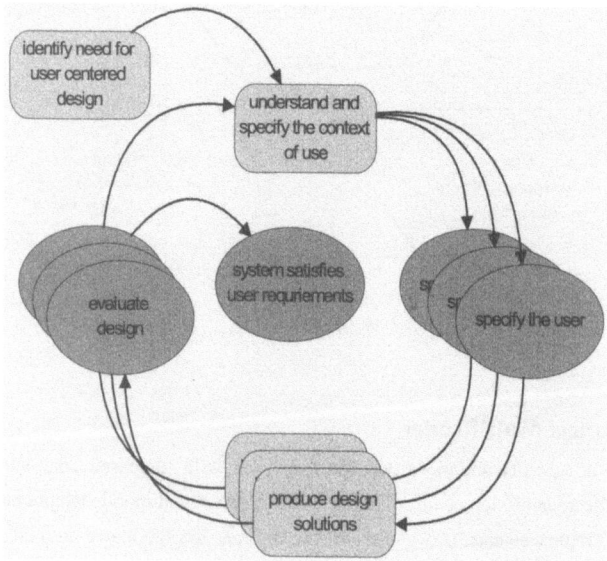

Figure 3: Initial iterative user-centred design lifecycle for heterogeneous user group

However, one of the problems when trying to "design for everyone" an iterative user-centred lifecycle with numerous, heterogeneous user groups is how to deal with the design lifecycle for all the different groups. As can be seen from Figure 3, this involves running numerous parallel user needs, design and evaluation processes. This model makes certain problems apparent:

- creating parallel systems producing conflicting requirements
- creation and management of the different versions required.

For a discussion of iterative development of MultiReader documents see Petrie et al., 2003. The creation of different versions is based on XML documents and transformation using XSLT in a client/Server system and in the local application Reader software.

3.1 Personalisation of Multimedia Documents

Mark-up languages provide the technical capability to generate personalized versions of a multimedia document. Recommendations by W3C such as HTML and SMIL for interactive web pages parallel the development of industry standards for eBooks namely through the OpenEBook consortium[2].

Following the W3C approach the user agents allows for the personalisation of the user interface to suit the reader's needs. Table 3 describes the requirements by different user groups.

Presentation \ User Group	Blind	Partially Sighted	Deaf	Dyslexic
speech output	x	x		x
good descriptions of images and graphics	x			
audio descriptions in videos	x			
vary font style and size		x	x	x
vary text and background colour		x	x	x
enlargement of images, graphics and video		x		
text or graphic output for speech and auditory signals			x	
extensive use of pictorial, graphic and video material			x	
sign language translations			x	
increase line spacing, line length			x	x
word-by-word or sentence-by-sentence highlighting of text			x	x
presentation of information in short and simple "bite sized" chunks for ease of reading and comprehension			x	x

Table 3: Summary of User Requirements

Some requirements are concerned with the provision of additional contents, such as the need for sign language and audio description in videos, which require consideration of time-dependent media and identification of temporal intervals. Highlighting of text is such an interval and clarifies the synchronisation of different time-dependent media in non-trivial and requires additional mark-up techniques—described by Petrie, et al., 2002 in a selection task of

[2] www.openebook.org

a multimedia tour guide, although the combination of HTML and SMIL still lacks a clear model of the integration of animation with keyboard-based input.

3.2 Document Architecture

We propose instead a variety of additional mark-up documents which would:

- define the profile of a user (profile DTD)
- define a particular selection of document nodes (tour DTD)
- define session-based properties such as zoom factor and highlighting speed (session DTD)
- define navigational enhancement (Topic Map DTD)

Figure 4 describes the overall document architecture of a MultiReader document. In order to implement selection of a tour within a multimedia tour guide a graphical map has been developed which can be magnified and hence is more accessible to readers with low vision. The Scalable Vector Graphics DTD is aware of the needs of blind people, but current user agents provide little support based on the enriched graphics. Figure 5 shows such a map.

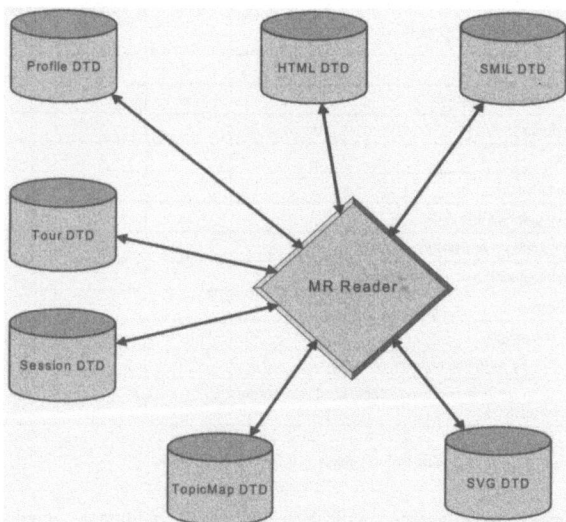

Figure 4: Overall architecture of MultiReader multimedia documents

One approach that makes maps more accessible to blind people is being investigated on the basis of a Phantom force-feedback device, while 2.5D relief maps may be combined with 3D small scale models of sightseeing stops as described by Springsguth and Weber, 2003.

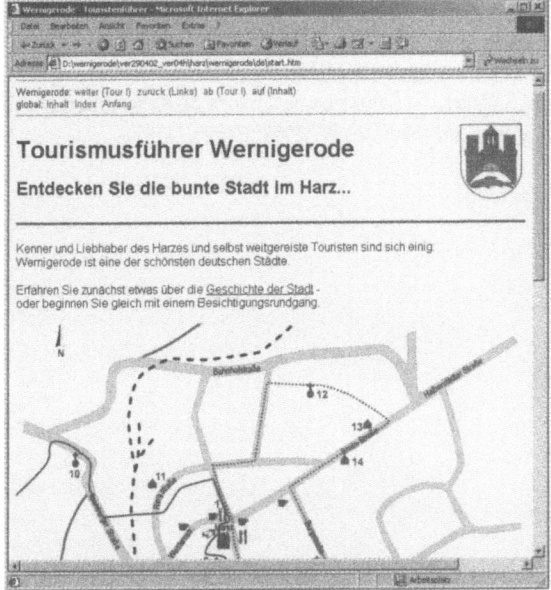

Figure 5: Tour selection

4   Concluding Remarks

Because the MMC is still in its developing stages, it is somewhat early to evaluate degree program as both staff and organisation of MMC is growing. Currently, MMC staff has identified drawbacks relating to

- the extensive amount of coursework
- the varied student backgrounds
- lack of periods to make up for student and faculty illness

Greater course diversity and selection may assuage the first two issues, while intensifying individual student mentoring could deal with the final issue.

The MMC intends to develop an independently-staffed Centre for multimedia communication and eBusiness (Berghammer, Weber, 2003) with a focus on industrial collaborations.

References

Berghammer, R; Weber, G. (2003) Multimedia Campus Kiel – Ein Konzept für die Zukunft?, in Keil-Slawik (ed.) *Tagungsband Quality in Education Forum*, (Dortmund, 21.-22.11.2002), in print.

Petrie, H.; Fisher, W.; Gladstone, K.; Rundle, C.; Pyfers, L.; van den Eijde, O.; Weber, G. (2002) Navigation in multimedia documents for print-disabled readers, in *Proc. HCI International*, June 22.-28., 2003, Crete), in print.

Petrie, H.; Langer, I.; Weber, G.; Fisher, W.; Gladstone, K.; Rundle, C.; Pyfers, L. (2002) U-
niversal Interfaces to Multimedia Documents, *International Conference on Multimodal
User Interfaces*, IEEE, (Pittsburg, 14-18.Okt. 2002), S. 319-324.

Springsguth, Chr.; Weber, G. (2003) Design Issues of Relief Maps for Haptic Displays, in
Proc. HCI International (June 22.-28., 2003, Crete), in print.

Media Informatics at the University of Ulm

Michael Weber

Introduction

The city of Ulm has maintained a tradition in design since the 1950s. Components of what was once the Hochschule für Gestaltung (HfG) founded by Max Bill, now stand as the existing school of design and successor of the Bauhaus, focusing not only on graphics and design, but also film production and research at the University of Ulm. Moreover, the HfG is well represented by the likes of Max Bense, Otl Aicher, Hans Gugelot, Nick Röhricht, Alexander Kluge, and Edgar Reitz. Indeed, many HfG teachers and former students continued on to live and work in Ulm, and foster a growing reputation in design.

In 1969—well after the HfG was forced to close due to financial difficulties, the University of Ulm was founded as a medical and natural science university, which expanded in the late eighties to include engineering (esp. electrical engineering) and informatics. In 1996 the computer science department began reviving aspects of the HfG design program in combination with the emergent field of media and specifically, media-related informatics. "Media engineering and media design" (*Medientechnik und Gestaltung*) was initially offered as a minor to explore the topic as well as test student acceptance. The re-emergence of the HfG—partially owned by the university, as a media development and research institute enabled the media engineering and design minor to begin in the fall of 1997.

Needless to say, the results of the test were tremendously successful, with approximately 40 percent of computer science students chosing to minor in Medientechnik und Gestaltung. At times, up to 60 students were enrolled in a given course, which lead to a three shift model in the design classes necessitating small-group work. Interestingly, there was a marked increase in female enrolment in these courses relative to other computer science courses. One could almost say, if a woman is studying computer science, it must be *Medientechnik und Gestaltung*.

Finally, a full degree in Media Informatics at the University of Ulm—requiring an eighth group (two professors and assistants) to cover the additional teaching load and establish research, was reviewed and approved by the ministry. Courses commenced in the fall of 2000 with 100 students enrolled from over 400 applicants.

Study Plan and Profile

Students who had enrolled in the Media Informatics minor displayed certain characteristics:

- A central affinity for design and the more creative aspects of computer science, such as human computer interaction, as well as cognitive and psychological theory.
- A lack of interest in theoretical and technical computer science or mathematics.

Thus, the Media Informatics curriculum was adapted to reflect these tendencies, and because a majority of the curriculum is computer science or media-related informatics subjects, it was simple to maintain the original computer science degree, while placing an emphasis on a sound computer science education for Media Informatics students.

Coursework for the degree is separated into (1) basic studies and (2) advanced studies, which typically take nine semesters to finish. The first two years of basic studies are necessarily quite regulated for all students, while advanced studies are much more flexible with minimal contingencies. The basic courses are outlined in the following, with media informatics courses shaded, with the others corresponding to the traditional computer science program.

Semester 1	Computer Science 1	Linear Algebra	Analysis	Design 1
Semester 2	Computer Science 2	Higher Mathematics	Interactive Systems	Design 2
Semester 3	Software Engineering Lab	Humanities	Introduction to Media Informatics	Economics
Semester 4	Technical Informatics	Theoretical Informatics	Seminar	Media Psychology and Didactics

Table 1: Coursework during the first four semesters in Media Informatics at Ulm

During the advanced coursework in the latter portion of the degree, students are free to select from all courses currently offered by the faculty, given that a minimum of 16 to 32 credits (80 are covered in total) cover media informatics topics such as multimedia, computer graphics, computer vision, image processing, dialog systems, or web engineering. Additionally, students must choose an applied subject such as: interactive systems, film and video, simulation and animation or media psychology. The applied subjects are usually organized as project-oriented courses spanning three consecutive semesters. Two practical works, seminars, and finally a half year thesis bring the program to a total of 240 credits.

First Experiences

The first enrolled class is now in their sixth semester, while subsequent applications remain continuously above the 100-student capacity at roughly 400 applicants per year, with admission determined by high-school exam grades.

Thus far, media informatics courses have been effectively conducted as highly personal and intensive hands-on twenty-person courses, with notable positive effects in future advanced coursework. Indeed, because traditional computer science and media informatics students are relatively undistinguished early on, many of the faculty differentiate media informatics students via the increased quality of their 'products', presentations, and papers. For example, media informatics students demonstrate a much higher sensibility towards user interfaces in advanced software engineering projects. In contrast, traditional computer science students who lack certain basics, may continue on relatively undetected given the structure of courses, with improvement depending largely on self-discipline: a relatively unreliable process in struggling students. Lastly, if a mere quarter of students applying for the media informatics program are admitted based on high school exam performance, they can be expected to—and do, perform better than the traditional computer science students entering without any grade-based admission control.

Research Program

Currently, the computer science department is composed of nineteen faculty—all more or less involved in areas related to media informatics, with two faculty in the department of media informatics, where research is conducted in multimedia, computer graphics and aspects of human computer interaction with an emphasis on collaborative work. Specifically: (1) the neuroinformatics department provides significant research in the areas of computer vision, image processing and analysis, and cognitive aspects of human-machine interaction; (2) the department for distributed systems focuses on multimedia-capable operating systems and quality-of-service architectures; (3) the AI department studies multi-agent systems; (4) the database and information systems department pursues research in multimedia information systems as well as metadata approaches; (5) e-learning projects are jointly performed by the media informatics, artificial intelligence, and software engineering departments; (6) the educational psychology group is involved in research about self-regulated learning and how this can be improved by user interface designs and metaphors; and lastly, (7) the faculty for electrical engineering focuses on speech processing and generation of natural language to form a true multi modal spectrum of HCI-research.

Conclusion

Within three years, it is clear that the diploma program in media informatics at Ulm has been a complete success: with applications far exceeding the quota and a drop-out rate slightly lower than the traditional computer science degree. Although media informatics maintains an intensive workload of project-oriented studies that are rather expensive in an environment of decreasing academic funding, the combination of design and media-related informatics continues the tradition of the HfG Ulm in the new and highly relevant domains of media and media-related informatics.

Contributors with Papers

Elisabeth André
University of Augsburg
Department of Computer Science
E-Mail: andre@interactive-multimedia.de
P. 19

Klemens Böhm
University of Magdeburg
Department of Computer Science
E-Mail: klemens.boehm@iti.cs.uni-magdeburg.de
P. 91

Jana Dittmann
University of Magdeburg
Department of Computer Science
E-Mail: jana.dittmann@iti.cs.uni-magdeburg.de
P. 57

Rainer Groh
University of Dresden
Department of Computer Science
E-Mail: rg5@inf.tu-dresden.de
P. 9

Nick Halper
University of Magdeburg
Department of Computer Science
E-Mail: nick@isg.cs.uni-magdeburg.de
P. 67

Christoph S. Herrmann
University of Magdeburg
Department of Biological Psychology
E-Mail: Christoph.Herrmann@nat.uni-magdeburg.de
Pp. 67, 91

Heinrich Hussmann
University of Munich
Department of Computer Science
E-Mail: Heinrich.Hussmann@informatik.uni-muenchen.de
P. 15

Roland Jesse
University of Magdeburg
Department of Computer Science
E-Mail: jesse@isg.cs.uni-magdeburg.de
P. 79

Rainer Kohlschmidt
University of Rostock
Department of Engineering and Information Technology
E-Mail: rainer.kohlschmidt@etechnik.uni-rostock.de
P. 99

Frank Lesske
University of Magdeburg
Department of Politics
E-Mail: frank.lesske@gse-w.uni-magdeburg.de
P. 57

Volker Linneweber
University of Magdeburg
Department of Psychology
E-Mail: Linneweber@gse-w.uni-magdeburg.de
P. 67

Winfried Marotzki
University of Magdeburg
Department of Education
E-Mail: winfried@marotzki.de
P. iv, 57

Mara Mellin
University of Magdeburg
Department of Psychology
E-Mail: maramellin@hotmail.com
P. 67

Frieder Nake
University of Bremen
Department of Computer Science
E-Mail: nake@informatik.uni-bremen.de
P. 1

Ian J. Pitt
University College Cork, Ireland
Department of Computer Science
E-Mail: i.pitt@cs.ucc.ie
P. 103

Wolfgang Prinz
Fraunhofer FIT and
University of Aachen
Department of Computer Science
E-Mail: wolfgang.prinz@fit.fraunhofer.de
P. 25

René Rosenbaum
University of Rostock
Department of Computer Science
E-Mail: rrosen@informatik.uni-rostock.de
P. 99

Gunter Saake
University of Magdeburg
Department of Computer Science
E-Mail: saake@iti.cs.uni-magdeburg.de
P. 79

Klaus Sachs-Hombach
University of Magdeburg
Department of Computer Science
E-Mail: ksh@isg.cs.uni-magdeburg.de
P. 37

Kai-Uwe Sattler
University of Magdeburg
Department of Computer Science
E-Mail: kus@iti.cs.uni-magdeburg.de
P. 79

Jörg R.S. Schirra
University of Magdeburg
Department of Computer Science
E-Mail: joerg@isg.cs.uni-magdeburg.de
P. 37

Ingo Schmitt
University of Magdeburg
Department of Computer Science
E-Mail: schmitt@iti.cs.uni-magdeburg.de
P. 91

Jochen Schneider
University of Magdeburg
Department of Computer Science
E-Mail: josch@isg.cs.uni-magdeburg.de
Pp. iv, 37

Heidrun Schumann
University of Rostock
Department of Computer Science
E-Mail: schumann@informatik.uni-rostock.de
P. 99

Thomas Strothotte
University of Magdeburg
Department of Computer Science
E-Mail: tstr@isg.cs.uni-magdeburg.de
Pp. iv, 51, 67, 79

Klaus-D. Tönnies
University of Magdeburg
Department of Computer Science
E-Mail: klaus@isg.cs.uni-magdeburg.de
P. 91

Gerhard Weber
Multimedia Campus Kiel GmbH
E-Mail: g.weber@mmc-kiel.com
P. 111

Michael Weber
University of Ulm
Department of Computer Science
E-Mail: weber@informatik.uni-ulm.de
P. 121

Contributors without Papers

Jürgen Friedrich
University of Bremen
Department of Computer Science
E-Mail: friedrich@informatik.uni-bremen.de

Johannes Fromme
University of Magdeburg
Department of Education
E-Mail: johannes.fromme@gse-w.uni-magdeburg.de

Knut Hartmann
University of Magdeburg
Department of Computer Science
E-Mail: hartmann@isg.cs.uni-magdeburg.de

Alan Kay
Hewlett-Packard
HP Labs
E-Mail: Alan.Kay@squeakland.org

Maic Masuch
University of Magdeburg
Department of Computer Science
E-Mail: masuch@isg.cs.uni-magdeburg.de

Arnd-Michael Nohl
University of Magdeburg
Department of Education
E-Mail: Arnd-Michael.Nohl@gse-w.uni-magdeburg.de

Bernhard Preim
University of Magdeburg
Department of Computer Science
E-Mail: preim@isg.cs.uni-magdeburg.de

Lutz Priese
University of Koblenz/Landau
Department of Computer Science
E-Mail: priese@uni-koblenz.de

Heidi Schelhowe
University of Bremen
Department of Computer Science
E-Mail: schelhowe@informatik.uni-bremen.de

Stefan Schirra
University of Magdeburg
Department of Computer Science
E-Mail: stschirr@isg.cs.uni-magdeburg.de

Stefan Schlechtweg
University of Magdeburg
Department of Computer Science
E-Mail: stefans@isg.cs.uni-magdeburg.de

Ulrike Spierling
University of Applied Sciences of Erfurt
Department of Architecture
E-Mail: spierling@fh-erfurt.de